W9-CIN-719

THE BIGGEST LOSER

FITNESS
PROGRAM

NBC

THE BIGGEST LOSER

FITNESS
PROGRAM

**Fast, Safe, and Effective Workouts
to Target and Tone Your Trouble Spots
—Adapted from NBC's Hit Show**

The Biggest Loser **Experts and Cast**

with Maggie Greenwood-Robinson, PhD

Forewords by Jillian Michaels and Kim Lyons

Notice

This book is intended as a reference volume only, not as a medical manual. The information given here is designed to help you make informed decisions about your health. It is not intended as a substitute for any treatment that may have been prescribed by your doctor. If you suspect that you have a medical problem, we urge you to seek competent medical help. The information in this book is meant to supplement, not replace, proper exercise training. All forms of exercise pose some inherent risks. The editors and publisher advise readers to take full responsibility for their safety and know their limits. Before practicing the exercises in this book, be sure that your equipment is well-maintained, and do not take risks beyond your level of experience, aptitude, training, and fitness. The exercise and dietary programs in this book are not intended as a substitute for any exercise routine or dietary regimen that may have been prescribed by your doctor. As with all exercise and dietary programs, you should get your doctor's approval before beginning. Mention of specific companies, organizations, or authorities in this book does not imply endorsement by the author or publisher, nor does mention of specific companies, organizations, or authorities imply that they endorse this book, its author, or the publisher. Internet addresses and telephone numbers given in this book were accurate at the time it went to press.

© 2007 by Universal Studios Licensing LLLP. *The Biggest Loser*™ and NBC Studios, Inc. and Reveille LLC. All rights reserved.

All rights reserved. No part of this publication may be reproduced or transmitted in any form or by any means, electronic or mechanical, including photocopying, recording, or any other information storage and retrieval system, without the written permission of the publisher.

Rodale books may be purchased for business or promotional use or for special sales. For information, please write to: Special Markets Department, Rodale Inc., 733 Third Avenue, New York, NY 10017

Printed in the United States of America
Rodale Inc. makes every effort to use acid-free ⊗, recycled paper Ⓢ.

Book design by Christina Gaugler
Illustration on page 149 by Judy Newhouse
Portrait shots of Jillian Michaels by Joseph Puhy / Portrait shots of Kim Lyons by Per Bernal
Workout shots of Jillian Michaels and Kim Lyons by Per Bernal
All other photos by Trae Patton/Reveille.
Recipes on pages 159 to 162 are from *The Biggest Loser* and *The Biggest Loser Cookbook*.

The Library of Congress has cataloged the previous edition as follows:

Greenwood-Robinson, Maggie.
    The Biggest Loser fitness program : fast, safe, and effective workouts to target and tone your trouble spots-adapted from NBC's hit show! / the Biggest Loser experts and cast, with Maggie Greenwood-Robinson.
        p.   cm.
    Includes bibliographical references and index.
    ISBN-13 978–1–59486–695–1   paperback
    ISBN-10 1–59486–695–3   paperback
    1. Reducing exercises.   2. Weight loss.   3. Physical fitness.   I. Biggest loser (Television program)   II. Title.
RA781.6.G72   2007
613.2'5—dc22   2007025249

Direct, online version available August 2009:
ISBN-13: 978–1–60529–418–6

Distributed to the trade by Holtzbrinck Publishers

                                                        10   paperback
                    2   4   6   8   10   9   7   5   3   hardcover

We inspire and enable people to improve their lives and the world around them

For more of our products visit **rodalestore.com** or call 800-848-4735

Product Development & Direction:

Chad Bennett, Dave Broome, Cindy Chang, Neysa Gordon, Mark Koops, Kim Niemi

NBCU, Reveille, 25/7 Productions and 3Ball Productions would like to thank the many people who gave their time and energy to this project:

Jenna Alifante, Stephen Andrade, Dana Arnett, Sebastian Attie, Nancy N. Bailey, Shane Balazy, Erica Bello, *The Biggest Loser* contestants, Maria Bohe, Cindy Chang, Scot Chastain, Elayne Cilic, Marie Connolly, Dr. Michael Dansinger, Camilla Dhanak, Milissa Douponce, Leslie Duong, Jenny Ellis, Kat Elmore, John Farrell, Cheryl Forberg, Kurt Ford, Ariana Gadd, Jeff Gaspin, Chris Gaugler, Marc Graboff, Chris Grant, Maggie Greenwood-Robinson, Erica Gruen, Heather Halloway, Nancy Hancock, Libby Hansen, Bob Harper, Julie Harris, Kim Hedland, Shelli Hill, Dr. Robert Huizenga, Helen Jorda, Gary Kay, Allison Kaz, Dr. Jennifer Kerns, Jessica Kirby, Loretta Kraft, Chris Krogermeier, Laura Kuhn, Kellie Kulikowsky, Beth Lamb, Melissa Leffler, Michelle Llorens, Roni Lubliner, Kim Lyons, Carole MacDonal, Vince Manze, Rebecca Marks, Joaquin Mesa, Jillian Michaels, John Miller, Ann Morteo, Kam Naderi, Todd Nelson, Julie Nugent, Bill Ostroff, Howard Owens, Carole Panick, Joanne Park, Trae Patton, Liz Perl, Jerry Petry, Craig Plestis, Deri Reed, Chris Rhoads, Lee Rierson, Beth Roberts, J. D. Roth, Jessica Roth, Jennifer Scott, Robin Shallow, Ben Silverman, Hayley Sneiderman, Mitch Steele, Charles Steenveld, Lee Straus, Amy Super, Deborah Thomas, Matt Vassallo, Stacey Ward, Bob Wright, Yong Yam, Jeff Zucker

Contents

Dear Reader,

Welcome to the Biggest Loser lifestyle. I am so thrilled that you have been inspired by the journey of our Biggest Loser contestants.

In life we are the sum total of the choices we make. So let me commend you for purchasing this book! What an exciting choice you are making to get control of your health and thus your life.

It's likely that you will not find the weight-loss process to be "easy"—I have yet to meet the person who has. The path to wellness is a strenuous one, but when you make a commitment to a healthy path and honor it as best you can, the road rises up to meet you.

The joy you will reap from a healthy life is worth every drop of blood, sweat, and tears you could ever shed. No, no, don't panic. This book isn't gonna make you bleed, but it will definitely make you sweat— lots and lots—and maybe shed a tear or two.

Change is a kind of private revolution. Each time you learn something new, you must readjust the whole framework of your knowledge and being. It seems to me that one is forced to make inner and outer readjustments all one's life. The process never ends. And yet, for many people, this is a continuing problem because they have an innate fear of change. The new unknown becomes something hostile in their minds to be feared. It's true that change can at times be painful, but pain makes us grow in incredible ways. To quote one of my favorite poets, "pain cracks the shell that holds our understanding"—that is, the understanding of our capabilities, strengths, and ultimately our destiny.

The purpose of the Biggest Loser lifestyle goes beyond the physical. It is about challenging yourself, getting a little uncomfortable, and allowing the treasures of your infinite depths and potential to be revealed.

Remember, courage is more exhilarating than fear and in the long run it's easier.

You do not have to become a hero overnight. Just a step at a time, meeting each challenge as it comes.

I will leave you with this thought before you begin reading: What has been in our lives has absolutely nothing to do with what can be. It's time to let go of those old ideas and philosophies of "I can't" and shift your focus to "I can." Use the knowledge and the tools in this book to help you on your own personal journey towards wellness. Like the Biggest Loser contestants, you too have the strength inside to stare down and overcome any obstacle and live the life that you choose and deserve.

Good journey,
Jillian Michaels

Dear Reader,

When I began weight training 12 years ago, I never dreamed it would change my life and lead me down the path of changing my clients' lives. I never dreamed that living a healthy lifestyle would give me mental and physical strength and the confidence to overcome insecurities. More important, I never dreamed that I would have the opportunity to give back what I have learned to millions of viewers through *The Biggest Loser!*

One of the most common questions I'm asked by people just like you is "What is the secret to losing weight?" I've been asked that question hundreds of times—in the grocery store, on the street, in the gym, and at the mall. It doesn't matter where I go; people want to know the big secret of *The Biggest Loser.* My answer is simple: commitment, dedication, direction! You have to commit to making a change, dedicate the time to fit workouts into your routine, and set weekly goals to achieve. I know that's easier said than done in our too-busy lives, but trust me, it is well worth the journey! And by picking up this book, you have made the first step in that journey.

The Biggest Loser Fitness Program is not your everyday "how-to" book. It is also a book of inspirational stories of people who have made the decision to save their lives through the good old-fashioned way of exercise and proper nutrition. The exercises illustrated in this book have stood the test of time and have been proven to be effective by everyday people just like you.

This book not only contains tips from people who have "been there, done that," but it also tells the stories of the way lives were changed forever. Whether you have 10 pounds or 200 pounds to lose, this book will give you the inspiration and proof that exercise can and will change your life forever.

These exercises aren't all going to be easy—and that is OK! Learn to laugh when something seems impossible, cry if you need to cry, or let out a grunt of frustration while you're learning. The key is to *keep* trying and to enjoy improving with every workout. I've spent hours laughing and crying with my team members over these very exercises!

Whether your goal is to look good in your birthday suit or to be healthy in order to keep up with your kids and grandkids, there is no better time than right now to get started. Believe in yourself and start today—you are worth it! Now . . . drop and give me 20!

Kim Lyons

Introduction

Have you watched *The Biggest Loser* and heard the call? Better listen to it: Now just might be the time to lose those pounds . . . take control of your health . . . and start changing the way you feel about yourself.

With the Biggest Loser fitness program—and your determination—you can kick-start your fat-burning power and begin shedding pounds at a safe and steady rate. You'll see attractive, substantial changes in your shape and appearance within a few weeks. Looking good is important because it makes a statement about who you are and how you feel about yourself. And just think of the energy, health, and confidence you'll have as a result. No matter how diet- or workout-weary you are, the Biggest Loser fitness program will perk you up and give you renewed hope. It is designed to recharge your metabolism, burn calories faster, and help you feel and look better than ever in no time. It is based on the same drop-weight, firm-up exercise principles you've seen on *The Biggest Loser.*

NBC's wildly popular reality show has taken overweight Americans from all walks of life, who are fed up with bad diets and weight-loss gimmicks and who are seriously ready to lose weight, and helped them achieve jaw-dropping transformations. The show's premise: Overweight contestants are divided into teams and square off in a weight-loss competition of dieting, exercise, hard-to-resist temptations, and grueling physical challenges. Contestants from each team are eliminated along the way, and at the end of the season, the remaining contestant who has dropped the greatest percentage of body weight wins the grand prize of $250,000. In just the first three seasons of the show, the contestants on *The Biggest Loser* collectively lost a staggering 6,469 pounds.

And for some, losing those pounds was a matter of life or death.

Kai Hibbard, a Season Three finalist, for example, had dangerously high cholesterol—a forecast of heart trouble—and blood pressure levels of 140/90 and sometimes greater—a leading risk factor for heart disease and stroke. But she beat those numbers back with healthy eating and exercise—and no medication. Her cholesterol

dropped by 113 points, and her blood pressure eased down to 112/64.

Another touching example is Erik Chopin's unhealthy-to-healthy story (Erik was the Season Three winner). He was diagnosed with full-blown type 2 diabetes, which is the third leading cause of death in this country. Erik carried so much fat on his frame that his body was not able to use its own insulin, the hormone responsible for ushering sugar into cells for nourishment—a condition formally known as *insulin resistance*. Consequently, sugar (glucose) kept stockpiling in his body, making him diabetic and putting him at risk for complications of diabetes such as heart disease, eye disease, nerve damage, and kidney disease. By exercising on a regular basis and eating healthy foods, Erik shed the weight he needed to (all 214

Kai Hibbard, Alaska

Status: **Finalist, Season Three**
Currently: **A newlywed who teaches aerobics and is earning her personal trainer certification**
Age: **27**
Height: **5 feet, 5 inches**
Hometown: **Eagle River, Alaska**
Occupation: **Law Student**
Starting Weight: **262 pounds**
Total Weight Loss: **118 pounds**

Erik Chopin, New York

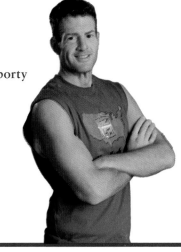

Status: WINNER, Season Three
Currently: Cruising town in a new sporty (and small!) blue car
Age: 35
Height: 6 feet, 2 inches
Hometown: West Islip, New York
Occupation: Deli Dad
Starting Weight: 407 pounds
Total Weight Loss: 214 pounds

pounds of it!) and his body responded by becoming perfectly sensitive to insulin once again. His fasting blood sugar went down from 144 to a normal level of 93. As one of the show's physicians, Dr. Robert Huizenga, told Erik, "That's nothing short of miraculous!"

Miracles do happen on the show. They come in the form of pounds lost and health gained. They come in the form of before-and-after photos that are not only amazing but utterly inspiring. More than anything, they come in the form of small-scale successes like the contestants' victories over self-destructive habits—emotional overeating, poor portion control, inactivity, smoking, and others—that so many of us can relate to. It's no wonder *The Biggest Loser* and its contestants have found such a huge audience. They are us!

Inspired by these amazing results, season after

season, Biggest Loser fans have started changing their lives once and for all. All over the world, people have started their own Biggest Loser competitions in hospitals, offices, and schools, pushing each other toward healthier lives. The Biggest Loser phenomenon has even spawned a series of best-selling books and workout DVDs as well as an online club (www.BiggestLoserClub.com), a powerful community geared toward helping you get the slender, toned, fit, and healthy body you want—for life. It's at this club that you'll find menus, as well as support and advice from experts, trainers, and real-life people who had hundreds of pounds to lose and did it—really did it! You can also meet the cast in a personal and riveting way. You'll read their stories and learn their breaking points and how they turned it all around.

The same success can happen to you. Although

Brian Starkey, Tennessee

Status: Eliminated player, winner of $100,000 prize, Season Three

Currently: Speaking to others about healthy living, when not hiking or riding mountain bikes with his family

Age: 33

Height: 5 feet, 11 inches

Hometown: Knoxville, Tennessee

Occupation: Stay-at-Home Dad

Starting Weight: 308 pounds

Total Weight Loss: 156 pounds

each of you who picks up this book has a different story and different reasons to get in shape, you all have something in common. You are reading this book to get healthy, lose weight, become more active, and transform your life. But before you lose weight, you actually have to gain something. You have to gain focus on yourself. From the very first page of this book to the last, you are going to move yourself to the top of your to-do list because being healthy is really the most generous thing you can do for yourself and for the people who love you.

This book is an in-depth, easy-to-follow guide to getting worthwhile results from exercise. But not just any type of exercise. The Biggest Loser fitness program is a special type of workout that involves your whole body in one muscle-working, heart-pumping, flexibility-building, calorie-burning workout. Most of us need to work on everything—muscles, joints, and heart—to get in shape, especially if we haven't exercised in a while or are getting older. Accordingly, this program spot-shapes your body in various zones; confers an aerobic element for heart and lung fitness; promotes "functional training" to help your body handle real-life daily activities; gives you the flexibility to move gracefully and silence creaky joints; and does all of this in one single, seamless workout that you can complete in less than an hour. The Biggest Loser fitness program is the answer to one of the biggest exercise dilemmas we all contend with: not enough time to exercise. You don't need to buy any expensive equipment, either. You can do this workout right in the comfort and convenience of your own living room, bedroom, or other place in your home.

Research has proven time and again that people who exercise are healthier in general. Given that simple fact, it makes sense to be physically active. Exercise fights heart disease, high blood pressure, obesity, diabetes, depression, mental sluggishness, arthritis, and a host of other conditions and ailments. When you're in good physical shape, your body will be better able to handle whatever comes its way. Clearly, what matters to your waistband matters a whole lot to your health. Never exercised before? Trust us, you can do this. There's no longer any excuse to sit on the sidelines. Use it or lose it has arrived!

What Will It Take?

You have to start somewhere, even if it's just 15 minutes a day. There is a practical lesson to be learned from the Biggest Loser contestants and their workouts and it can be summed up in a word: *muscle.*

Every season, the contestants on the show concentrate on developing and building muscle—something you'll learn to do, too. This is one of the "secrets" to driving weight loss and keeping those pounds from coming back. Most people lose lean mass (mostly muscle and water) as well as fat when they lose weight. This is especially true if they diet by cutting calories without exercising. When the weight comes back, most of it is fat. With each loss/gain cycle, the percentage of lean mass decreases and percentage of fat increases, all of which slows your metabolism.

For every pound of fat you gain, your body burns a mere 2 calories a day, compared to an average of 50 calories for each pound of muscle you put on. So if you lost 5 pounds of muscle by overly restricting calories and not exercising, you're burning about 250 fewer calories a day. Muscle simply burns more calories than fat tissue, so the more muscle you have, the more calories you burn, even at rest. It makes perfect sense to have muscle's automatic fat-burner working in your favor.

Once you reach your goal weight, you will burn more calories at that weight and be better positioned to keep the weight off. The show's contestants have proven it! Dr. Huizenga, a medical expert on *The Biggest Loser*, has tracked the weight, fat, lean tissue, and other body-composition changes in each contestant, starting in the first season. His preliminary results are encouraging: A year after the end of the first season, contestants were still doing well. These contestants originally lost an average of 25 percent of their body weight over 22 weeks. One year after the end of the show, they had maintained an average weight loss of 22.6 percent. That's pretty impressive when you consider the bleak statistics on people regaining weight after a program of diet

Poppi Kramer, New Jersey

Status: **Winner of the 50 States Prize**

Currently: **Working as a health correspondent for the Maury Povich Show**

Age: **35**

Height: **5 feet, 2 inches**

Hometown: **River Edge, New Jersey**

Occupation: **Actress/Stand-Up Comic**

Starting Weight: **232 pounds**

Total Weight Loss: **117 pounds**

and exercise: Of those shedding 10 percent of their body weight—considered a significant amount—only about 20 percent will keep it off in the first year.

As the Biggest Loser contestants have learned, for greater fat loss you've got to develop muscle for maximum fat-burning, sustained weight loss, and lasting weight control. The Biggest Loser fitness program is geared toward building more muscle and curbing muscle loss, so that you can develop a sleeker, firmer body and not gather pounds as the years go on. If you're a woman, you don't have to worry about "bulking up," either. You don't have the hormonal makeup to build big muscles, but you will develop sleek, sexy curves. Just look at Suzy Preston, Drea Baptiste, or Amy Hildreth if you don't believe us!

The Biggest Loser Fitness Program at Home

Perhaps the ultimate question: Can I replicate at home the sensational results I see on the show? For sure, the key to successful weight loss is making meaningful and sustainable lifestyle changes. But please know: You don't have to be on reality TV to enjoy the same successes achieved by the Biggest Loser contestants. Remember Adrian Kortesmaki from North Dakota and Jaron Tate from Arkansas in Season Three? Eliminated early, they returned to the ranch for one episode *to show how well they were doing at home.* Both lost a greater percentage of body weight than any of the noneliminated contestants! In fact, one contestant (Heather Hansen) remarked: "I couldn't believe it. Adrian and Jaron have better percentages than we do!"

Heather's observation speaks to the fact that you can be a "biggest loser" by following Biggest Loser principles at home. Jaron, in fact, lost half a person! At the start, he tipped the scales at 323 pounds, lost 163 pounds, and now weighs a lean, defined 160 pounds. He has totally embraced a fitness lifestyle, too. Jaron's fitness goal is to compete in the Ironman Triathlon: An accomplishment he hopes will inspire not only his extended family, where obesity and diabetes run rampant, but America as well.

Despite being overweight, Adrian was a former athlete in high school and was voted "Most Inspirational" by her teammates. In college, however, her weight problems really kicked in when the freshman 15 became the freshman 60. She started at 227 pounds, dropped 66 pounds, and is on her way to her goal weight of 125. Not only that, she has dreams of racing in the Birkebeiner, a 51-kilometer Nordic ski race.

And let's not forget Poppi Kramer, the witty, engaging but struggling stand-up comic from New Jersey, who was one of 36 Biggest Losers who competed at home instead of on the Biggest Loser ranch. Poppi went on to win $50,000 after being the biggest loser who stayed at home. Her main reason for wanting to lose weight was, in her own words, "I couldn't breathe." Weighing in at 232 pounds, then continuing her get-trim regimen at home, Poppi lost 117 pounds. Today, she is a svelte 115 pounds and able to fit into her goal outfit—premium designer jeans and a fitted black-leather jacket. In the last few years Poppi's father was diagnosed with leukemia. He is

Suzy Preston, Washington

Status: **Finalist, Season Two**
Currently: **Married to Biggest Loser winner Matt Hoover and new mom of Rex Timothy Hoover**
Age: **31**
Height: **5 feet, 4 inches**
Hometown: **Des Moines, Washington**
Occupation: **Hairdresser**
Starting Weight: **227**
Total Weight Loss: **95 pounds**

Matt Hoover, Iowa

Status: **WINNER, Season Two**

Currently: **Touring the country giving motivational speeches about healthy living; married to Suzy Preston, and new dad of Rex Timothy Hoover**

Age: 31

Height: 5 feet 10 inches

Hometown: Marion, Iowa

Occupation: Motivational Speaker

Starting Weight: **339 pounds**

Total Weight Loss: **182 pounds**

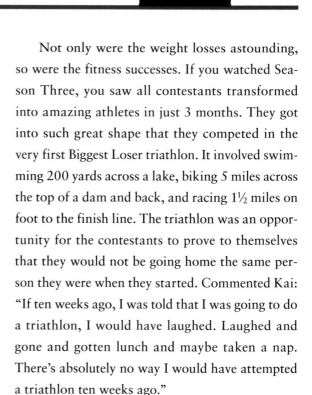

currently in remission, and Poppi performs at a leukemia benefit each year. Her goal is to get fit enough to run a fundraising marathon in his honor.

The evidence that you can be a "biggest loser" at home is weighty! Every season, there is one contestant who wins the $100,000 consolation prize by beating out the other eliminated contestants on the finale. Remember Dave Fioravanti from Season One, who reduced from 260 pounds down to 183 pounds? How about Pete Thomas from Season Two, who dropped from 407 pounds to 216 pounds (an incredible loss of 191 pounds)? Or Brian Starkey from Season Three, who dropped from 308 pounds down to 152—over half his weight? Their transformations happened mostly at home, in the real world.

Not only were the weight losses astounding, so were the fitness successes. If you watched Season Three, you saw all contestants transformed into amazing athletes in just 3 months. They got into such great shape that they competed in the very first Biggest Loser triathlon. It involved swimming 200 yards across a lake, biking 5 miles across the top of a dam and back, and racing 1½ miles on foot to the finish line. The triathlon was an opportunity for the contestants to prove to themselves that they would not be going home the same person they were when they started. Commented Kai: "If ten weeks ago, I was told that I was going to do a triathlon, I would have laughed. Laughed and gone and gotten lunch and maybe taken a nap. There's absolutely no way I would have attempted a triathlon ten weeks ago."

These contestants—people just like you—are living proof that no one is doomed to a life of being overweight and inactive. Like the Biggest Loser contestants or the Biggest Loser club members, who have lost 50, 75, or more than 100 pounds, you can do it, too.

It starts with the right frame of mind—using a certain type of energy, focus, and thinking process to get what you want. Most people who have tried over and over again to get in shape have failed many times at those attempts. As a result, they have a "failure mentality." Can you relate?

If so, you've got to get over that mentality. How badly do you want to feel good about yourself? Are you willing to do the work to get the results you want? The fact is, you can do it this time, if you want. Think of changes you've successfully made in your job, in your family, or in any endeavor in which you gained new knowledge or skills. Deciding to exercise and lose weight is just another change in your day-to-day life that can be mastered. The power to make it happen begins with your thoughts, which create the action to change what you most desire.

There's a powerful message in all the Biggest Loser success stories: You can take back control of your life and embrace a new, healthy lifestyle. Becoming more active requires changing long-standing habits. And if you've got a lot of weight to lose, chances are, you've got a lot of changes to make. It will take continuous effort and motivation.

Start by believing that you have the power to control your body and your destiny. The wonderful part is that as you begin to change your body, this power will grow stronger. Every day that you eat more thoughtfully, every day that you follow the Biggest Loser fitness program, every day that you're good to yourself, you'll gain a sense of control, self-mastery, and empowerment. The Biggest Loser fitness program can make a world of difference in your life. Don't waste any more time feeling bad about the way you look or cheating yourself out of being physically fit. Take control of your body and your life today.

Taking It Off

If you've never been introduced, let us present *circuit training,* the guiding exercise principle behind the Biggest Loser fitness program. In a nutshell, it is a style of exercise in which you perform one set of an exercise and immediately move to the next one with only several seconds of rest in between, alternating muscle groups as you work. Aimed at losing both weight and inches, circuit training trims your body in measurable ways, enhances heart and lung fitness, helps you feel healthier and happier, and is perfect for beginners and experienced exercisers alike. The exercises and the actual workout will be outlined for you in the chapters to come.

Circuit training is the best way to burn fat fast—and does so in a couple of important ways. First, the exercises are strength-training moves, in which you lift a dumbbell or use exercise tubing, move your own bodyweight, or work with a stability ball. Strength training adds body-defining muscle, and the more muscle you have, the faster your metabolism. A faster metabolism helps accelerate your fat loss.

As good as strength training is for fat loss and metabolic health, it also helps harden your bones. In middle-aged women especially, bones get less dense and more prone to breaking due to a decrease in physical activity and hormonal changes associated with menopause. But you may be able to slow down or halt this process altogether with the Biggest Loser fitness program. That's because any exercise that strengthens muscles also seems to slow the rate of bone loss. Stronger muscles and bones make real-life activities such as lifting, carrying, or walking upstairs easier by reducing your risk of injury and fatigue. The Biggest Loser fitness program is designed with all of these aspects of "functional fitness" in mind.

Matt Hoover's Exercise Tip

Each day is a new day. It doesn't matter how hard you worked yesterday or how hard you didn't work yesterday, you have to pick it back up and keep going.

The second way circuit training burns fat is through aerobics. By moving fairly quickly through your exercises, you create an aerobic effect. Aerobic activity burns fat by increasing your body's fat-burning enzymes and improving oxygen delivery to tissues. Your heart rate remains elevated throughout the entire circuit, providing calorie-burning benefits while you do the exercises. This continuous motion is one of the aspects of circuit training that makes such a difference between being trim and forever fat.

Aside from the physical workout and the benefits of getting in better shape, expect to feel an emotional rejuvenation, too. Researchers have measured psychological responses to circuit training and have discovered that fairly substantial emotional changes occurred when people circuit train. They're less anxious, less depressed, less prone to anger, and more resistant to stress. Clearly, there is a lot to be gained from this type of workout when you consider the emotional and psychological benefits.

One of the other advantages you'll love about this workout is that it saves something few of us have much of: precious time. You'll be able to complete the workout in as little as 30 minutes. Squeezing time into your schedule to work out will no longer be a stumbling block for you. This time-efficient total body workout puts your weight-loss goals within reach.

The Science behind Circuit Training

The benefits mentioned above have been well documented and substantiated in the scientific literature. Let's take a closer look at what science says about fitness and what circuit training will do for you.

Burn Lots of Calories

Because so many muscles are involved in circuit training, you burn more calories than you do in a regular session of moderate weight lifting. Weight lifting burns anywhere from 211 calories to 259 calories an hour, depending on your body weight. But a circuit-training routine, according to published research, burns between 368 and 540 calories an hour! That's a significant difference which can translate into significant fat loss.

Burn More Fat

Circuit training has a fat-burning effect on the body that is achieved through a mechanism called *EPOC* (excess post-exercise oxygen consumption). EPOC refers to the extra calories you burn once your workout is over. Yes, you burn plenty of calories during your workout to energize your muscles. But you continue to do so even after you've stopped. Circuit training has been shown in some studies to boost EPOC for as long as 38 hours after your workout—longer than traditional weight lifting will do. With circuit training, you'll be moving fairly rapidly from set to set, with very short rest intervals, and your heart rate stays elevated. The net effect is to make the workout intense. The more intense your workout, the longer you burn calories afterward.

Suzy Preston's Exercise Tip

I set my alarm clock at 4:30 a.m. most days to get to the gym by 5 a.m. I have a gym buddy, a good friend, and I show up faithfully, knowing my pal is there waiting for me.

Shrink Belly Fat

Where you are plump influences more than just your appearance. It directly affects your health. People with an excess of abdominal fat (a waist size greater than 40 inches for men, and 35 inches for women) are high-risk candidates for diabetes, heart disease, and even some cancers. In addition to diet, you can trim the excess fat around your waist by exercising. Studies have shown that 8 weeks of circuit training can provide increased abdominal and trunk fat loss. And best of all, reduced fat in your abdomen is associated with a reduced risk of disease.

Develop Muscle Everywhere

When you perform the Biggest Loser fitness program, you may feel like you're using muscles you didn't know you had, particularly around your waist, buttocks, thighs, back, and arms. But you'll be pleased with the results. Practically every significant piece of research on circuit training has found that it changes your body composition for the better, giving you more balanced proportions, less body fat, greater muscle tone and development, and more.

Enhance Your Functional Fitness

You want to be strong and agile enough to carry your groceries, pick up your kids, flip a mattress, help a friend move furniture, or play your favorite sport well. But as we get older, our joints begin to stiffen up, and unexercised muscles peter out. Both conditions compromise our *functional fitness* (the ability to perform everyday activities with strength, flexibility, and balance), but the good news is that circuit training will improve it. In a study at Florida Atlantic University, physical function, mobility, flexibility, and balance increased in 119 elderly men and women who performed a circuit-training routine three times a week for 12 weeks. Pain decreased, and so did doctors' visits. Many of the exercises you'll do in the Biggest Loser fitness program concentrate on your "core." Technically, the term *core* includes the lumbo-pelvic-hip complex and the thoracic and cervical spine. In plain English, that just means everything except

Ryan Kelly's Exercise Tip

Don't blame the fact that you don't exercise on the fact that you don't have a trainer. You can have the best trainer in the world, but he or she can't exercise for you. So you just have to get out there and do it.

your arms and legs. When we refer to the core, we are talking about the deep muscles below your abs that help stabilize your body when you're moving on unstable surfaces or at varying speeds. All movement is based on these stabilizing muscles. Strengthening them is what enables you to generate power effectively and perform activities of daily living without aches, pain, weakness, or compromised mobility.

Control Blood Sugar

Exercise is one of the lifestyle tools now known to help control type 2 diabetes and quite possibly reverse its course. A study conducted at the University of Western Australia underscores this exercise connection. In studying the effect of an 8-week circuit-training program on the health of 16 subjects with type 2 diabetes, researchers found that this method of exercise improved blood sugar control, enhanced heart-lung fitness, developed muscular strength, increased muscle, and reduced body fat. A number of other studies have found similar results.

Modify Risk Factors for Heart Disease

People used to think that any exercise that didn't have you pounding the pavement wouldn't help your heart. If you weren't running or jogging, you weren't going anywhere. Not anymore. Now we know that low-impact exercise like walking and circuit training can do your heart a world of good, according to accumulating data. A Swedish study, for example, put 151 middle-aged men and women with risk factors for heart disease (abnormal blood fats, high blood pressure, obesity, or type 2 diabetes) on a supervised circuit-training program three times a week for 3 months, then did a follow-up study with the group after 1 year. The reduction in risk factors was quite apparent: The participants decreased their blood pressure, lost weight, trimmed their waistlines, and reduced their triglycerides. Those with type 2 diabetes reduced something called *glycolated hemoglobin,* which measures average blood sugar levels over a 3-month period and is the only accurate measure of overall diabetes control.

The science behind circuit training is convincing—but so are the results you've seen week after week by watching the contestants of *The Biggest Loser* get into better and better shape. So—if you want your best body ever—let's get in gear to do the workout they do.

What You'll Need

With the Biggest Loser fitness program, you can exercise at home, inexpensively turning any room in your house into a functioning fitness center with the following fun-to-use and easy-to-store equipment:

Dumbbells. These are short metal bars with either changeable plates on the end or fixed plates. They are designed to be held in one hand. You'll want to gradually up your poundages, since challenging your muscles to lift more weight produces

Don't Write Off Joining a Gym!

As you work through the Biggest Loser fitness program, you'll learn moves that can be done at the gym as well as at home. All well-equipped fitness centers have the tools needed for this program, and you'll also find additional options to spice up your routine. Consider a salsa dancing class to boost your cardio routine, or yoga instruction to work on your flexibility. The options are limitless!

the body-changing results you want. Have sets of dumbbells on hand weighing 5, 10, 15, 20, and 25 pounds so that you can gradually increase the weights you use. These simple and inexpensive workout tools will work virtually every part of your body. Many of the exercises in the Biggest Loser fitness program use dumbbells.

Exercising tubing. This equipment consists of tubes of flexible, stretchable rubber with handles on the ends for applying controlled resistance on specific muscles or groups of muscles. Exercise tubing comes in several different levels of difficulty, determined by the elasticity and by the color of the band. You may want to have two or three

Shannon Mullen's Exercise Tip

If you work at a desk job where you sit all day, make sure you get up and move. Why not take the stairs to get to your office? I do, and I work on the 11th floor.

bands on hand in order to increase your resistance. Because they are so portable, you can pack your exercising tubing and take them when you travel.

Exercise mat. This is a must for the home gym. It will cushion you from the hard floor when doing abdominal exercises, floor exercises, and warmup stretches.

Stability ball. Some of the exercises incorporate a stability ball into the routine. Working out with a stability ball is an incredible way to sculpt your entire body. Aside from being inexpensive, this exercise tool is versatile and fun to use. You can strengthen and stretch nearly every muscle in your body (including your core), while improving balance, coordination, and posture. This piece of equipment comes in different sizes based on your height. A proper fit will help you work your way to a firmer body with better posture, more defined abs, and even less back pain. Here is a guide:

Your Height	Proper Sizing
Under 4' 6"	30-cm (12") ball
4' 6" to 5' 0"	45-cm (18") ball
5' 1" to 5'7"	55-cm (22") ball
5' 8" to 6' 2"	65-cm (26") ball
Over 6' 2"	75-cm (30") ball

Medicine ball. This exercise tool is a heavy ball about the size of a volleyball that generally comes in weights from 2 to 15 pounds. It can be used with many different exercises, particularly to strengthen your core muscles.

Xerdisc. This is a circular cushion made of plastic that can be used for balance training or upper- or lower-body conditioning and is generally used for advanced exercises.

Ankle weights. These are light weights (usually between 1 and 5 pounds) that you can strap to your ankles for adding extra challenge and intensity to certain exercises. However, these weights are not to be used when walking, jogging, or running due to the high potential for leg and back injuries.

Heart-rate monitor. To keep your fat-burning fires stoked while you build muscle, you'll want to maintain a heart rate between 80 percent and 85 percent of your maximum heart rate. To determine your maximum heart rate, subtract your age from 220. Calculating 80 percent and 85 percent of this number provides you with your *target heart-rate zone*. Wear a heart-rate monitor to help keep you there. You might be thinking that wearing a heart-rate monitor is like splitting hairs. Don't you just do the routine, burn calories, and lose weight? Well, you might. But if you don't wear a heart-rate monitor, you might not either. If you are exercising too intensely, you won't be dipping into fat stores at all—you could even be burning muscle. And if you're not elevating your heart rate sufficiently, you might not know. Using a heart-rate monitor takes all the guesswork out of your workouts. It's also a lot of fun, and it gives you immediate feedback on the effort you're making. There are several different brands out there. Good heart-rate monitors can be found at most sporting good stores and start at around $50.

Jennifer Eisenbarth's Exercise Tip

I like to tell myself I won't make any personal phone calls until after I work out. That gets me going.

Erik Chopin's Exercise Tip

Instead of watching the clock during cardio workouts, listen to music.

Workout Safety

Every time you exercise, you may feel some degree of muscle soreness. This soreness is a normal muscle response to unaccustomed exercise, stimulation after neglect, or to the new stimulus of circuit training. Muscle soreness is actually a good thing, as long as it is not too severe, because it is a sign that you adequately stressed your muscle fibers. In about 48 hours, you muscles will repair themselves and become stronger. Even so, there are ways to minimize muscle soreness:

- Warm up thoroughly with the Biggest Loser fitness program warmup exercises in the next chapter. These will increase your body temperature, including your muscle temperature, and make your body more resistant to muscle soreness.

Ken Coleman's Exercise Tip

Every day, walk for at least 30 minutes to 1 hour at a medium to fast pace.

- Perform the cooldown stretches following your workout. These increase blood flow to and from the exercised muscles, ensuring more delivery of nutrients and hormones for recovery and repair, as well as flushing out chemical waste products that lead to soreness.

- Enjoy a nice hot bath following your workout. It's all the better if you can apply water-jet massage from a Jacuzzi tub. Research indicates that water-jet massage increases the release of proteins from muscle tissue into the blood and helps reduce muscle soreness after a taxing workout.

- Don't let muscle soreness sideline you; stick to your workout schedule. If you stop working out, you'll only get sore again the next time you exercise. As long as you properly warm up, any sore body parts will be massaged by the repetitions of the exercising, stimulating blood flow through the sore muscle for a healing effect.

Muscle soreness is one thing, but how can you tell the difference between soreness and an injury to your body? If you injure yourself during a workout, you'll usually feel a sharp or incapacitating pain, or visible swelling. Or if you've inflamed a body part, you'll feel a dull, nagging pain in that area. Either way, you'll know intuitively that something is wrong. Here's how to avoid workout injuries:

- We can't say it too many times in too many ways: Warm up properly prior to exercising; cool down afterward! The Biggest Loser fitness program warmup exercises (see Chapter 2) are designed to elevate your muscle temperature slightly and prepare your body for the workout. Muscles are like furnaces. They produce heat and this makes them more pliable, like putty, and in that state, your body is adequately prepared to exercise. Afterward, the cooldown exercises focus on stretching for flexibility, joint health, and muscle protection.

- Follow all exercise instructions carefully and concentrate on proper form (explained in the section on page 10).

Nelson Potter's Exercise Tip

If you really want to lose weight, up the exercise and keep a steady, consistent pace.

Melinda Suttle's Exercise Tip

Never put off exercise. It's always worth it.

- Never jerk or pull a weight abruptly; this can lead to torn ligaments and joint trauma.
- Don't be overenthusiastic and lift weights that are clearly too heavy for you.
- Listen to your body's signals that you may be doing too much or exercising incorrectly. If something doesn't feel right, stop immediately. Signs that you're overtaxing your body include muscle and joint pain and swelling and fatigue. In addition, women may stop menstruating. Fortunately, the Biggest Loser fitness program sets reasonable limits so that you won't overdo it. You'll work out 30 to 40 minutes three or four times week on nonconsecutive days, giving your body adequate time for rest and repair.

Proper Exercise Form

If you want your workouts to count—that is, produce a fitter, healthier, more attractive body—then you'll want to understand and practice proper exercise form. Proper form when extending and retracting your muscles optimizes calorie burn and results. Neglecting form causes you to work out inefficiently. Poor form can also mean unnecessary stress on joints, misalignment, and injury. Exercise with a rounded back and one day something's going to snap. Lock your elbows at the end of a chest fly and your joints are going to protest. Even if you've been able to get away with less-than-perfect form and are injury free, you're not getting the most, if anything, out of your workout.

So, what exactly is good exercise form? Here are a few of the basics of form to keep in mind:

- Keep your back straight but not arched. If your back is curved while you add a weighted load to an exercise, you are placing an unhealthy strain on your back.
- Activate your core (trunk muscles) when performing any movement. The more stable your core, the less risk of injury.
- Isolate the muscle group you are working. Make sure you can feel those muscles—and only those

Lezlye Donahue's Exercise Tip

Wear a proper sports bra.

muscles—during an exercise. That means, for instance, if you're doing a biceps curl, the only body part that should be moving is the portion of your arm between your hand and elbow. Your back, shoulders, and legs should not get in on the act. That means no swaying, rocking, or any other ways of "helping" that weight up.

- Choose a grip when using dumbbells that feels most comfortable and natural to you. Your grip should be firm but not too tight. Squeezing the equipment wastes valuable energy that should be exerted in the exercise.

- Always control the exercise—no rapid, jerky movements, which place harmful stress on the joints, ligaments, and tendons. Jerky motions actually give the weight so much impetus that it practically glides to the midpoint of the repetition, using little muscular force to get there. As a result, the muscles encounter limited resistance. Without resistance, muscles aren't properly challenged and may not respond as well. If you can't lift the weight without jerking it, then it is too heavy. Try a lighter weight. Strict style and technique are more important than the amount of weight you lift.

- At the midpoint or top of the exercise, pause for a second to tense your muscles. Then lower the weight slowly again, accentuating the negative portion of the lift. Your muscles thus get maximum stimulation from the exercise.

Patty Gonzalez's Exercise Tip

Concentrate on the muscle you are working.

- Breathe naturally as you exercise. Never hold your breath. Holding your breath cuts oxygen supply to the blood and, coupled with the exertion of the lift, could cause lightheadedness or fainting.

How to Select Your Starting Weights

It's best to choose a weight with which you're able to control the tempo of the lift and the range of motion. Because your repetitions will usually be around 12 per set, select a weight with which 10 reps would be nearing failure, the point at which you cannot complete another repetition. Another way to look at it: If you can complete 12 to 15 repetitions of any exercise without any difficulty, the resistance is definitely too light. The key is to *challenge* your muscles—make them feel like they're working—in order to stimulate changes in your body.

When to Increase the Resistance

Making your muscles work harder each time you exercise means progressively upping your poundages or doing more repetitions. Muscles adapt very quickly to stresses placed on them. For continual progress, you must always add weight to exercise, do more repetitions with the same weight, or both. Whenever an exercise feels too easy, increase the weights or repetitions. Another strategy to up the ante: Most of the exercises in the Biggest Loser fitness program have advanced versions. Progress to these as you become more fit. Increasing your effort during each workout makes your muscles become firmer and stronger.

Planning Your Workout Schedule

The best schedule is every other day, or at least three times a week on nonconsecutive days, alter-

nating your workout days with rest days. How you schedule your workout depends on your personal situation. Some people might exercise on Monday, Wednesday, and Friday; someone else might choose Tuesday, Thursday, and Saturday. Or you can simply alternate days through the week if you prefer to work out more than three times a week.

Proper Hydration

When you exercise, you sweat. And when you sweat, you lose fluid. Our bodies are mostly water, so even a slight shortage can make you *dehydrated,* which describes an insufficient amount of water in your system. Dehydration causes a reduction in blood volume, which means less oxygen gets to your working muscles; it negatively affects your heart rate; and it compromises energy systems in your muscles. There's a drop in your energy levels, so you don't get as much from your workout when you're dehydrated.

Recent studies show that water may play a role in the regulation of your metabolism—your body's calorie-burning engine. For one thing, if you become dehydrated, your metabolism tends to slow down, meaning that you won't burn as many calories as normal while at rest. In addition, ample water may reduce appetite and control food intake by making you feel full. Water also dilutes sodium

Nicole Michalik's Exercise Tip

When doing aerobic work on a machine, cover the timer on the machine with a towel; this makes the time left seem less daunting.

levels in the body, making it the best remedy for fluid retention.

You can avoid dehydration—and the accompanying drop in energy and metabolism—by taking steps to protect yourself ahead of time. Here are some guidelines for staying hydrated:

- Upon rising, drink 2 cups of water to help cleanse and detoxify your system. You tend to be dehydrated in the morning, so this is a good time to replace fluids.
- Although the traditional recommendation is to drink a minimum of eight 8-ounce glasses of water a day—which is a good move—it's more

Isabeau Miller's Exercise Tip

If you don't break a sweat, you aren't working hard enough.

accurate to base your water intake on your body weight. For example, try to drink at least half your body weight in ounces daily. If you weigh 200 pounds, your daily intake would be least 100 ounces. That's 12½ glasses (8 ounces each) a day.

- Drink water during your workout. You should consume 6 to 8 ounces of water every 15 to 20 minutes while exercising.
- Water your body after exercise. Have two 8-ounce glasses of water to restore fluids.
- Limit caffeinated soda, tea, and coffee, as well as alcohol. All of these have a diuretic effect, causing fluid loss from your body. If you enjoy caffeine or alcohol, follow them up with a water chaser just to stay in balance.
- If you feel hungry, you might actually be thirsty. How can you tell the difference? Simply drink a glass of water if you think you're hungry. If the water satisfies you, you were thirsty, not hungry.
- Don't like plain water? Flavor a pitcher of plain water with herbs like mint or basil, or slices of citrus fruits or cucumber.

- Watch liquid calories in general. If you're not careful, it's quite easy to get a lot of excess calories from beverages. Because they're liquid, those calories go down easily, and we can ingest a lot of them without even knowing it. The most common culprits are sodas and fruit juices. An average can of soda alone can have up to 60 grams of sugar—that's the same amount of sugar in four pieces of bread. That said, you'll want to curtail sodas and fruit juices and learn to enjoy water instead.

You Can Exercise Only So Much Away

Along with the Biggest Loser fitness program, you'll want to follow the Biggest Loser diet, summarized for you in Chapter 8 and covered in detail in a previous book, *The Biggest Loser*. A lot of people mistakenly think that if they exercise, they can eat anything they want. So they work out like maniacs and then wonder why they never make any progress. Or worse still, they wonder why they seem to be gaining weight even with all the time they spend exercising. The problem is that while exercise is necessary for losing body fat, you can easily sabotage all that hard work with just a little extra food.

For example, one circuit-training session, depending on your weight, intensity, and body composition, burns hundreds of calories. To lose body fat, you have to create a caloric deficit. So if you sneak a few cookies in—say, eight cookies, 2 inches in diameter, that's about 400 calories. If you only burned 400 calories working out, you're only breaking even. You just wiped out that calorie deficit, and you're not making any progress. If you eat 12 cookies, then you've got to work your way out of an *excess* of 200 calories.

So don't forget that nutrition is at least half of the fitness equation. In fact, some trainers will tell you it is 70 percent of the equation. Others say it's up to 90 percent! But let's leave that open to debate. Just know that you can only expect results if you pay attention to both your eating and exercise habits.

Going Forward

In the pages that follow, you'll learn to master the exercises that make up the Biggest Loser fitness program. Within each chapter, you'll be introduced to a series of recommended exercises, with clear instructions, covering a different area of the body (upper body, core, and lower body), along with chapters on warming up and cooling down. In Chapter 7, you'll put it all together with routines designed to reshape your body and build a totally new you, inside and out. Because nutrition is so important, you'll find the Biggest Loser diet in Chapter 8.

It is best if you read through the entire book first to get familiar with the exercises, the workout, and the diet before you start. Be sure to read the contestant tips scattered throughout the text, too; they're meant to motivate and keep you on track. After all, the biggest losers have been where you are and know what it takes to overcome obstacles, stay focused, and keep going until all that unwanted fat is gone.

The Biggest Loser fitness program is something you can do, no matter what your schedule, present state of conditioning, or weight. Stick with it and you'll see fat dropping off your body and muscles developing in all the right places. And once you experience the wonderful results, you'll want to continue this type of workout for life.

Warming Up for Weight Loss

You've heard the universal recommendation to warm up before you work out. But if you're like many people, you may pass over this step because you feel pressed for time, or think that it's not really that important. So why don't more of us warm up? Good question!

Warming Up Is Important

Maybe warmups need a good ad campaign. An ad for warming up would tell you that it burns calories, enhances your fat-burning potential, prevents injuries, and more. By not warming up, you do miss out on many important advantages. So please don't go skipping on to the next chapter, proclaiming you've "heard it all before." There are some body-benefiting reasons to

warm up that you may not have considered. When you warm up properly, you will do the following.

Burn Extra Calories

For your warmup, the Biggest Loser fitness program recommends 10 minutes of light aerobic-type activity, consisting of several different moves, to prep your body for circuit training. You'll move at a leisurely pace—say 50 percent of your maximum heart rate. In that 10-minute span of time, you can expend up to 100 calories. When it comes to exerting energy, every little bit counts.

Matt Hoover's Exercise Tip

Learn to work around exercise-related injuries. While I was on the ranch, I pulled muscles on both my quads and my hamstrings. Before, those injuries would make me quit and set me back for months. But I learned that if I can't exercise my legs, I can still exercise my back, my arms, or my abs. A little injury doesn't have to affect everything.

Mobilize Sugar More Efficiently

Throughout the full 10 minutes of your warmup, your body will tap initially into sugar (glucose in the blood and glycogen in the muscles) for energy. By the time you begin your circuit routine, you'll have less sugar to spare, so your body will dip into its fat stores for energy much earlier. The advantage—you guessed it—more fat is burned.

Improve Exercise Performance

Think about what it's like to start your car's engine when it's cold. It performs poorly, right? Well, muscles are the same way; they don't work well until they reach the proper temperature. The temperature of muscle tissue rises about 3.6°F during your warmup, enough to produce sweating. Warming up also increases blood flow to your tissues, so that more oxygen and more nutrients (including fat) are channeled to your muscles for fuel. Increased blood flow also helps remove waste products from muscles, such as lactic acid, that burn-producing chemical that makes you want to quit. Finally, your warmup speeds up neural responses. Nerve impulses travel faster, improving your motor skills, coordination, reaction time, and agility. Warmed-up muscles move faster and generate more force than cold muscles and they burn more energy—which means your body is better primed to lose pounds.

Prevent Injuries

If your muscles are cold and stiff and you go full-throttle into your exercise routine, you're inviting injury on a couple of fronts. Your muscles shouldn't be used until they're warm and pliable. But in addition, when you warm up properly, raising your muscle temperature, your body begins to lubricate your joints for easier movement and your muscle tissue becomes more elastic. This is important for strength-training exercises in which you'll need to move a weight or resistance through a full range of motion. All of these physiological responses reduce the risk of overstretching or tearing muscle fibers and connective tissue. Also, if you begin a workout

TRAINER TIP:
BOB HARPER

If I'm free in the afternoon, I love to get outside and hike with my dog, Frank, who's a great companion. We hike; we don't walk. He's strong; he can run beside me on a bike.

without a warmup, you may provoke an irregular heart rhythm. In studies of healthy people, abnormal heart rhythms were found in those who exercised intensely without warming up, but disappeared when an appropriate warmup was included in their exercise routine.

But what if you do get injured? Does an injury sabotage your weight-loss efforts? Not necessarily. During Heather Hansen's audition for *The Biggest Loser*, she jogged in place for hours, raising her knees as high as she could to impress the producers that they could count on her to win. Once on the ranch, she paid a price for her competitiveness: a torn calf muscle, bursitis in her knees, and mild tendonitis in her quads. Trainer Kim Lyons guided her toward lower-impact workouts. "If you injure your lower body, there's always something else you can do," Kim explains. "I suggested that Heather try the gentler recumbent bike, elliptical trainer, or rowing machine while she healed." Of course, if you suffer from an injury, be sure to see your doctor or another medical professional.

Protect Your Immune System

Here's a little-known fact: Sudden all-out exercise (without warming up first) floods your body with stress hormones that can weaken your immune system and make you more susceptible to illness.

Your body doesn't like the shock of sudden exercise, so you've got to ease yourself into it by warming up first. That way, you'll help protect your immune defenses and prevent colds, flu, and infections.

Prevent Exercise-Induced Headaches

Some people are prone to *exertion headaches* that kick in shortly after vigorous activity like weight training. Don't worry, though: This type of headache is rare and usually short-lived, lasting anywhere from 5 minutes to as long as 48 hours in some cases. Although there may be multiple causes, an exertion headache is triggered by sudden dilations in blood vessels. You can reduce your chance of having a workout headache by warming up properly and staying well hydrated and well fueled and getting a good night's sleep every evening. Of course, if you get an exertion headache for the first time, or a headache that feels worse than you've ever experienced, call your physician immediately.

Get You in the Right Frame of Mind

Just as warming up prepares your body for physical activity, it also prepares your mind. The warmups you'll do as part of the Biggest Loser fitness program are rhythmic—a type of movement that increases alpha-wave activity in the brain, which produces a calm, focused state similar to meditation. This doesn't mean you'll feel like taking a nap or sitting lotus-style to meditate, but rather gives you laser-sharp mental concentration for your workout. Your mind is more likely to veer away from negative things or intrusive thoughts that can interfere with a productive workout. There's a powerful mind-body connection at work here that you can use to your advantage.

The Four Biggest Myths about Warming Up

Before moving on to the warmup exercises in the Biggest Loser fitness program, here are the four biggest warmup myths that circulate among exercisers. These myths need to be blown out of the water if you want to have a productive, results-producing workout and get the body you want.

TRAINER TIP:
KIM LYONS

Invest in a good pair of workout shoes. Not only is it important for your feet, but it is a good "get moving" reminder!

Adrian Kortesmaki's Exercise Tip

Don't compare yourself with your formerly fit self. Pretend you are starting from the beginning. Focus on how fit and healthy you're going to be.

Myth #1: Stretching is the best way to warm up before exercise.

Fact: Stretching is *not* the optimum way to warm up, particularly before any type of strength training or weight lifting, because your muscles are cold. Stretching cold muscles reduces the strength of muscle contractions and increases your odds of pulling or tearing a muscle. Light aerobic exercise is the best way to warm up, because it gets your muscles warm and pliable, plus increases blood flow. Then, when you do stretch, do it slowly and deliberately and stretch no further than you can hold for 5 seconds. And don't bounce. Bouncing makes your muscles contract more to protect themselves and they can tear too easily.

Myth #2: I don't need to warm up.

Fact: Not warming up is one of the biggest exercise mistakes anyone can make. It's like asking someone to drive a car around the block when they've never driven before. They can injure themselves. Warming up has numerous benefits, discussed above. Keep in mind, too, that a proper warmup enhances the efficiency and power of the working muscles—a benefit most people don't realize.

Myth #3: I don't need to warm up my legs because I use them all the time.

Fact: Not true. Your muscles are not being challenged in the same way by just walking around or normal, everyday movement. A proper warmup stimulates circulation to your legs, preparing them for your circuit-training workout. Bottom line: Don't neglect to warm up your legs.

Myth #4: I don't need to warm up if I'm exercising indoors.

Fact: Light aerobic activity produces heat in your muscles; the warmth of your home or gym does little to increase your internal temperature, regardless of how high the thermostat is.

Suzy Preston's Exercise Tip

I love to rollerblade and skateboard and hike. I try to do something outside every day, just for fun.

A Pre-Participation Fitness Quiz

Most people can and should exercise. Any amount of exercise you add to your daily routine will improve your life and your life expectancy. However, some may need to get their doctor's permission prior to beginning an exercise program, particularly if you have an unstable medical condition or injury. Before you start any exercise program or substantially increase your level of physical activity, be sure you're medically in good shape. Take the quiz below to make sure you're fit to exercise.

1. Have you ever been diagnosed with a heart condition or told that you should exercise only under a doctor's supervision?

2. Have you ever felt chest pain while exercising?

3. In the past month, have you ever felt chest pain when you were not exercising?

4. Do you ever lose your balance because of dizziness?

5. Do you have any joint or bone problems that could be aggravated by a change in your physical activity?

6. Are you taking any prescription medications for blood pressure or heart disease?

7. Is there any reason you know of that you should not exercise?

If you answered yes to one or more questions, if you are older than 40 and have been inactive, or if you are concerned about your health, talk to your doctor about increasing your physical activity or starting a new exercise program.

Adapted from the American College of Sports Medicine: Selecting and Using Home Weights.

Warmup Moves
for the Biggest Loser Fitness Program

Selected by the Biggest Loser trainers, the six warmup exercises described in the pages that follow prepare your muscles for the work they'll do in the circuit-training routine. You'll warm up by simply moving your body through Step Touches, Arm Raises, Simulated Jump Rope, and Marching in Place. There are also two smaller moves designed to loosen your neck and shoulders. All of these exercises are incorporated into your workout, explained in detail in Chapter 7, and provide a safe transition to circuit training.

Here are some extra guidelines:

- Read through each warmup description carefully; note the correct technique as demonstrated by the trainer in the photographs.
- Go at a comfortable pace; these moves are not designed to be aerobic.
- Have fun with your warmup; consider performing it to music.
- Never skimp on your warmup; it is time well spent, and your body will love you for it.

TRAINER TIP:
JILLIAN MICHAELS

As the Biggest Loser fitness program suggests, always warm up for 5 minutes with light cardio, then do your resistance training. Follow your routine by stretching. Don't stretch before you are warmed up because you could actually injure yourself that way.

Step Touches

For a full-body warmup, stand with your feet about shoulder-width apart. Step to the right with your right foot, and bring your left foot to meet it. Then quickly step to your left with your left foot, and bring your right foot to meet it. Repeat this sequence, picking up the pace. Keep your movements fluid, rhythmic, and controlled. Continue this step-touch motion for a full minute.

Arm Raises

To warm up your upper body, stand with your feet about shoulder-width apart. Hold your arms out in front of your shoulders and bend your elbows so that your hands are just at head level. Push your arms straight upward, and back down to the starting position. Repeat this sequence, picking up the pace. Continue this motion for a full minute.

Simulated Jump Rope

You don't need an actual jump rope for this warmup; just pretend you
have one. With your arms at your sides, rotate your wrists as if you
were throwing the jump rope over your head. Jump over the imaginary
rope with both feet simultaneously, using small jumping steps. When
jumping, hold your body erect, and jump upward no more than an inch
off the ground. Bend your knees just slightly upon impact. Continue
this motion for a full minute. For a lower-impact version, keep your
toes on the ground while raising your heels.

Shoulder Rolls

Stand with your feet a comfortable distance apart. Keep your arms at your sides. Roll your shoulders forward in a circle for 10 to 15 seconds. Then roll your shoulders backward in a circle for another 10 to 15 seconds. This is a good exercise to try throughout the day, particularly if you sit in front of a computer for hours at a time.

Neck Rolls

Stand with your feet a comfortable distance apart. Keep your arms at your sides or on your hips. Drop your head slowly forward, bringing your chin toward your chest. Lift your head and tilt your neck to the right toward your shoulders, then toward the left. Next, tilt your head back, then forward. Repeat this sequence for 30 seconds.

Marching in Place

Walking or marching in place is a great way to warm up your entire body. Simply stand with your feet together. Begin lifting your knees high, in alternating fashion. Combine marching in place with Arm Raises (page 25) for an even more comprehensive warmup. March in place for up to 5 minutes prior to starting your workout.

Next Up

In the next several chapters, you'll find step-by-step instructions on how to perform the exercises in the Biggest Loser fitness program. When performed consistently, you will get closer and closer to making changes in the way you look and feel. Take time to absorb and understand the essence of each exercise, and you'll get rid of fat and tighten and tone your body in record time.

Upper-Body Building and Sculpting

How do you think the Biggest Loser contestants managed to pull off feats like gathering beach sand to build tower-size hills, completing a grueling 1-mile race around the track wearing heavy weights on their bodies, or swimming in a triathlon? Answer: lots of upper-body strength!

Strength-wise, the contestants' workouts certainly equipped them for their weekly challenges, plus helped them develop chiseled, well-shaped physiques. Erik Chopin, the Biggest Loser winner from Season Three, immediately comes to mind. Here is a guy who was prepared to undergo gastric band surgery to shrink his stomach and slim down prior to being chosen for the show. "That's how hopeless I felt," says Erik, a family man and deli owner from West Islip, New York. "I felt like I needed to go for the surgery but, really, I'm so glad I didn't. I honestly knew the whole time, I'd be copping out." Well, 214 pounds later and lighter, Erik has built the bod of a Greek god, and nowhere was it more apparent than in his upper body.

Men typically love to focus on working their upper bodies, but women tend to spend time on their thighs and buttocks, often neglecting their back and shoulders. It's important for everyone to work upper and lower bodies equally for balance, symmetry, and functional strength. So: Fair warning! Do not skip any portion of your training, even if you feel like parts of your upper body are in reasonably good shape.

Targeted Muscles

The exercises covered in this chapter focus on the biceps, triceps, chest, shoulders, and back. The following muscle descriptions are given in the order in which you'll find them in the exercise directions.

Biceps. These are the muscles that work to flex your arms at the elbow. The little (or large) "ball" that forms is the biceps.

Triceps. About three-fourths of your upper arm is the triceps, a three-sided muscle that works to extend your arm and forearm (lower arm). This is an area of the body that tends to sag with age and lack of use.

Chest. The chest muscles, or *pectoral muscles*, are large, fan-shaped muscles that originate at the ribs and connect at the collarbone and sternum (breastbone). These muscles assist in pushing and throwing. Note to women: Independent of breast size, these muscles also create cleavage when well developed.

Shoulders. Shoulder muscles, or *deltoids*, consist of three parts: The anterior deltoid helps raise your arm forward and rotates it inward. The

medial deltoid raises your arm to the side and assists the other shoulder muscles. The posterior deltoid moves your arm back and rotates it outward. A shoulder-related muscle is the trapezius. It helps in overhead pushing actions and pulls your shoulders back and down (with the rhomboids). Biggest Loser trainer Kim Lyons notes, "In both men and women, well-developed shoulders help to create the illusion of a small waist and tapered hips—carving down into a 'V' shape, which puts the exclamation point on the body you are building every time you train."

What's Your "Goal Outfit"?

Each season on *The Biggest Loser*, contestants choose a "goal outfit"—a smaller-size garment, hung where it can be seen often, that serves as a visual reminder of the shape and size they want to achieve. For inspiration, why not choose your own goal outfit? Here are some ideas based on goal outfits chosen by the Biggest Loser cast in previous seasons:

- Slim-fit pair of jeans
- Bikini
- Fitted leather jacket
- Sexy dress or miniskirt
- Lingerie
- Smaller-size suit or slacks
- Any favorite outfit that used to fit
- Smaller-size work uniform

Back. Your back is a composite of different muscle groups: The trapezius assists in overhead actions, draws your shoulder blades back and down, and supports the shoulders when your arm is raised. The rhomboids, which lie beneath the trapezius, also pull the shoulder blades back and down and lift your torso. The latissimi dorsi (*lats*), which cover the low and mid portions of your back, assist in pulling your arms down and in toward your waist, and help stabilize your torso during the many activities that involve your arms. The attractiveness of a toned back and shoulders are lost if you slouch. Fortunately, you can help reverse poor posture with the right exercises for your upper body.

Go for It

A well-developed upper body is a work of art, with every muscle framing your physique and commanding attention. The multiple angles in which you train with these exercises are more than enough to bring rapid growth to every corner of your upper body. Using the workouts in Chapter 7, train your upper body as hard and as consistently as your abs and butt. Do that and we promise you an upper body that looks absolutely awesome.

The Upper-Body Exercises
for the Biggest Loser Fitness Program

With the following exercises, you'll build functional strength, burn fat, and re-sculpt your upper body. You'll also correct the imbalances that put the pain in your lower back and the slope in your shoulders, realigning your body so you can rehabilitate injuries, avoid future ones, and develop more body-shaping muscle all over. The circuit-training routine in Chapter 7 shows you how to integrate these exercises into your workout, so read the instructions here carefully.

Here are a few important safety tips and reminders for upper-body work:

- Read through each of the exercise descriptions carefully; note the correct exercise technique as demonstrated by the trainer in the photographs.
- With upper body exercises, a good rule of thumb is: shoulders back, chest up.
- During any upright exercise, such as shoulder presses or T-raises, avoid arching your back.
- During exercises in which you are lying on your back, such as chest presses or flies, keep your back flat.
- Keep your wrists in line with your elbows.
- Keep your head in line with your spine.

Biceps Curls

The Biceps Curl is perfect for sculpting, toning, and developing the front portion of your upper arms, and to some extent, your forearms. Nicely developed arms get a lot of attention and can be one of the most dramatic parts of the upper body. You'll need a pair of dumbbells that feel challenging when you lift them for 10 to 12 repetitions.

Positioning

Stand with your feet about shoulder-width apart. Grasp a dumbbell in each hand, with your palms facing front. Keep your elbows close to your sides, your back erect, and your abs tight throughout the exercise.

The Move

Flex at the elbows and curl the weights up toward your shoulders. Tense your biceps at the top of the exercise. Slowly lower the dumbbells back to the starting position (avoid letting your arms fall to the starting position). Repeat the exercise for the recommended number of repetitions.

Advanced Tips

An advanced technique is to perform curls while seated on a stability ball. Not only will you develop and strengthen your biceps, you'll also work your core (your abs and trunk muscles), since they are activated as you work to stay stable on the ball. You can also try raising one leg to increase your balance.

Bryan Washington's Exercise Tip

Keep your elbows close to body when curling; this better activates the muscle.

Hammer Curls

The Hammer Curl is a variation of the Biceps Curl explained on page 35 and is another way to work the biceps muscles of your arms.

Positioning

Grasp a dumbbell in each hand, and stand straight with your feet a comfortable distance apart. The palms of your hands should face your body. Keep your core muscles tight.

The Move

Bend your elbows and raise the dumbbells up toward your chest, making sure your palms face inward. Squeeze your biceps at the top of the movement. Lower slowly and repeat the exercise for the recommended number of repetitions.

Advanced Tip

As you did with the Biceps Curls, perform this exercise while seated on a stability ball. This makes the exercise harder and more challenging, plus works your core muscles.

Suzy Preston's Exercise Tip

I work with a trainer and we alternate days: upper body one day, lower body the next. If I miss some days due to my schedule, we'll try to touch on all parts.

Triceps Dips

The triceps muscle at the back of the arm is one of the most neglected on the human body, yet it makes up nearly three-fourths of your arm. You can be in fairly good shape, but if your triceps are soft or flabby, you immediately add the look of aging to your overall appearance. But don't worry: You can effectively firm up your triceps and recapture your youthful, fit look.

Positioning

For this exercise, all you need is a sturdy chair (or bench). Position yourself with your back facing the chair. Grasp the front of the chair's seat with your hands. Your forearms should be behind your back, facing forward, and your fingers should be pointing toward your feet. Extend your legs and hips forward on the floor so that they form a 45-degree angle with the floor. Your heels should help support your lower body.

The Move

Slowly bend your elbows, lowering your torso so that your hips are within a few inches of the floor. Once you reach this lowered position, push yourself back up slowly by straightening your arms. Lower and repeat for the recommended number of repetitions.

Advanced Tip

To make the exercise more challenging, place a weight plate or light dumbbell comfortably on your lap as you do the exercise.

Triceps Kickbacks

Another exercise for keeping the three-part triceps muscle in shape—and your arm jiggle-proof—is the Triceps Kickback. All you'll need for this exercise is a pair of dumbbells.

Positioning

Stand in the lunge position, with your left leg forward and hold a dumbbell in your right hand. Engage your abs to protect your lower back. Press your arm close against your side.

The Move

Bend your right elbow; then press the dumbbell backward in an arc until your arm is fully extended and parallel to the floor. In this position, lock your elbow and squeeze your triceps. Slowly return to the starting position and repeat the exercise for the suggested number of repetitions. Repeat with the other arm.

Advanced Tip

As you become stronger, you'll want to use heavier weights in order to challenge your triceps even more.

Push-Ups

The Push-Up is a classic exercise for shaping, developing, and lifting the chest, plus building overall body strength. It also sculpts and tones your arms.

Positioning

Kneel with your arms straight but not locked, wrists in line with your shoulders, fingertips facing forward, and your hands slightly wider than your shoulders. One at a time, extend your knees behind you until you are balanced with your knees on the floor (not shown).

The Move

Slowly lower your chest toward the floor. Bend your elbows and keep your palms in their fixed position. When your upper arms are parallel to the floor, press back up to starting position and repeat. Try not to bend or arch your back as you push up. Repeat the exercise for the recommended number of repetitions.

Advanced Tip

This exercise is more challenging if you perform it as shown. Lie chest down, with your hands at shoulder-level, palms flat on the floor. Keep your legs straight with your toes tucked under your feet. Straighten your arms as you press your body up from the floor. Try not to bend or arch your back.

Neil Tejwani's **Exercise Tip**

When doing Push-Ups, keep your butt low to the ground for a more effective chest workout.

Chest Flies

Here's an effective way to add detail and definition to your chest, plus give lift to this area and prevent sagging caused by time and aging. Strengthening your chest muscles also helps you stay functionally fit.

Positioning

Lie on your back on a mat, or on a standard flat exercise bench. Hold a dumbbell in each hand. Raise the dumbbells to an outstretched position just over your chest, with your arms straight and palms pointing in.

The Move

Bend your elbows slightly, and slowly lower your arms out to your sides. From this position, push the weights back up, following the same path you used to lower them. Slowly return to the starting position. Repeat the exercise for the suggested number of repetitions.

Advanced Tip

For an extra challenge, try this exercise on a stability ball. You'll work your chest and core at the same time.

Julie Hadden's Exercise Tip

I like doing Chest Flies lying on an exercise ball, as opposed to a bench. This works my core.

Chest Presses

This is a classic exercise for developing and strengthening your chest. When doing this move, you'll also indirectly stimulate the muscles of your front shoulders and your triceps, making this a versatile exercise for your upper body.

Positioning

Lie on your back on a mat or on a standard flat exercise bench. Hold a dumbbell in each hand, with elbows bent.

The Move

Raise the dumbbells to an outstretched position just over your chest, with your arms straight and palms pointing in. Then lower the dumbbells to the original position. Repeat the sequence for the suggested number of repetitions.

Advanced Tip

Do double-duty (chest and core muscles) by performing this exercise on a stability ball.

Amy Zimmer's Exercise Tip

Push your limits until you can't go any farther.

T-Raises

This exercise isolates the front portion of your shoulders, and you'll really feel it go to work. Strong shoulders enhance your performance in sports—particularly golf, racquet sports, and volleyball—where shoulder power is invaluable. Your arms will get some extra benefit from this exercise, too.

Positioning

Stand with your feet a comfortable distance apart. Grasp a light- to moderate-weight dumbbell in each hand, holding them with an overhand grip. Keep your arms straight and hold the weights at thigh level. Keep your back erect.

The Move

Slowly raise the dumbbells straight out in front of your body until they reach shoulder level. Then move your arms out to each side (you've just drawn a "T" in the air). Bring your arms back in, and lower them to the starting position. Repeat this sequence for the suggested number of repetitions.

Advanced Tip

As you become stronger, perform this exercise while standing on an unstable surface such as an Xerdisc or while seated on a stability ball. You'll give your core a terrific workout in addition to your shoulders and arms.

Shoulder Presses

By adding some muscle and a little more width to your shoulders, you can create the illusion of a smaller waistline and a more proportionate physique. Additionally, with an improved shoulder line, your posture will look better, helping you move with greater confidence. The Shoulder Press, which is an effective way to endow your shoulder line, will help you accomplish all of this.

Positioning

Stand with your feet a comfortable distance apart, with a dumbbell in each hand at head level, with your palms facing forward. Keep your back erect.

The Move

Press the weights upward to an overhead position. Lock your elbows at the top of the movement. Try not to lean forward. Slowly lower the dumbbells to the head-level position and repeat the exercise for the suggested number of repetitions.

Advanced Tip

The best way to turn this exercise into an advanced move is to stand on one foot as you complete the move. Switch feet halfway through each set.

TRAINER TIP:
JILLIAN MICHAELS

If you're a guy with a flabby chest, you have to burn off the fat with proper nutrition and exercise. Then, while you are losing the fat on top of the muscle, you can build the muscle to fill out your skin with exercises such as pushups, dumbbell presses, and cable flies.

Overhead Pullovers

Everyone should concentrate on building strength in the back. Doing so contributes to health, functional fitness, no-slump posture, and body symmetry (namely that athletic "V" shape that is so appealing and attractive). The Overhead Pullover is a multidimensional move for accomplishing each of these goals. Not only does it activate your back muscles, it also works your chest and triceps, making this a superior upper body exercise. All you need is a single dumbbell.

Positioning

It's helpful if you have a flat exercise bench. If not, a chair seat will do. Position your body crosswise to the bench or chair seat with your upper back resting on the bench or seat and your knees bent. Your body should actually form a right angle to the bench or seat. Hold a dumbbell with both hands over your body, with your arms extended.

The Move

Bend your elbows slightly, and slowly bring the dumbbell back over your head. Try to get a good stretch in your upper back muscles. Return the dumbbell to the starting position, and repeat the exercise for the suggested number of repetitions.

Advanced Tip

Listen to your body and increase the weight used in order to work your muscles to the point that they are sufficiently challenged.

Dead Lifts

One way you can help prevent lower back pain is to do exercises that strengthen this portion of your body. The Dead Lift is one of these moves. It also works your lower body.

Positioning

For equipment, you'll need two light dumbbells. Start with the weights on the floor directly in front of you. Take a shoulder-width stance.

The Move

Squat down until your knees are at about a 90-degree angle. Grasp the dumbbells with an "overhand grip"; that is, your hands curled over the handles of the dumbbells. Keep your back flat, your abs pulled in, and your neck neutral. Then press through your heels and extend your legs until you come to a standing position. Keep your shoulders back (squeeze your shoulder blades together) and your chest out. Guard against your lower back from rounding as you lift the weight from the start to the finish position. Remember to keep your arms straight throughout. Slowly repeat the movement.

Advanced Tip

Once you have mastered the correct form, increase the amount of weight you use on this exercise.

Bent-Over Row

No one wants to look a good deal older—which is what poor posture and slumped shoulders will do for you. By contrast, with a well-developed back, you'll create a more youthful posture and younger-than-your-real-age appearance. This great back-building exercise will help you get there, while indirectly working your biceps. All you need is one dumbbell.

Positioning

If possible, perform this exercise in front of a mirror to make sure you're positioned properly. Begin with the dumbbell on the floor. Place your left foot in front of your right and bend over so that your back is parallel to the floor, but with a slight arch. Your knees should be bent slightly. Engage your abs to protect your lower back. Grasp the weight with your right hand in an overhand grip.

The Move

Lift and pull the dumbbell into your chest. In this position, squeeze the muscles of your upper back. Lower the weight slowly to the starting position and continue for the suggested number of repetitions. Repeat the set with your other arm.

Advanced Tip

The best way to make this exercise more advanced is to increase the poundage you use. Don't stay stuck with the same weight.

Upper-Body Training Tips from the Trainers

- **Shoulders.** Work all parts of your shoulders evenly. Overdeveloping the front (anterior deltoids) shoulder and chest can make you look hunched over.—Kim Lyons

- **Shoulders.** It's more effective and safer to use lighter weights because the shoulder muscles are small. The heavier the weight, the tougher it is to keep the shoulder joint stable.—Jillian Michaels

- **Back.** The back is an area vulnerable to injury; work your back muscles no more than three times a week, with a rest day in between. If you're a beginner, go slowly when strengthening your back, particularly your lower back. Perform the lower number of repetitions suggested in the rep range for back exercises. Stop exercising if you feel any discomfort or pain.—Bob Harper

- **Arms.** If you want fully developed arms, you've got to work your biceps and your triceps. Many exercisers pay too much attention to their biceps, since these tend to be "show muscles." If you're only working the biceps, you're working less than half your arm. That's an imbalanced program.—Jillian Michaels

- **Chest.** Men love to work their pectorals (chest), but working out the chest can help women, too, by lifting sagging chests and breasts. In addition, chest muscles are essential in sports like tennis, free-style swimming, and any sport where you throw a ball.—Bob Harper

- **Overall.** Try to work your muscles in pairs, doing equal amounts of exercises with opposing muscle groups. If you're working your chest, you should also work your back, for example. If you're working your biceps, you should also work triceps.—Kim Lyons

4

Fit to the Core

If you're like most people, your main reasons for exercising are to be healthier, get in shape, and look better. All are worthy goals that you can achieve with an ongoing commitment to exercise and diet. But for a strong, defined, fit body, you've got to lay the right groundwork—and that means training your *core* muscles. Unless you've been stranded on a desert island, you've heard about core training. But what exactly does it mean, and why do you need to work your core?

With every move you make, there are muscles that keep you steady and stabilized, and other muscles that produce motion. Those that keep your body stable and balanced during movement, plus hold you upright, are your *core* muscles, found in your trunk. These muscles are the structural center of your body. Think of a baseball swing, a tennis backhand, carrying groceries, lifting objects, even simple movements like sitting or standing. All of these "functional" activities require activation of your core muscles so you can transfer power to your arms and legs from a solid foundation, while stabilizing your body.

It's important to add that poor posture compromises your core. Hunching over a desk, slouching in a chair, or walking around sloop-shouldered makes core muscles slack and will create a bulging belly. But correcting poor posture, along with exercises to retrain your core, will strengthen this part of your body and help you sculpt flat abs. Thus, with strong core muscles:

- Your posture is better.
- You'll have a healthy, limber spine.

- You'll have a leaner, more sculpted look.
- You'll walk taller (and look slimmer).
- You'll have better balance.
- Your body will react faster.
- You'll become stronger, more agile, and more flexible.
- You'll be less susceptible to many accidental and overuse injuries.

Targeted Muscles

The main muscles involved in stabilizing your core are those in your abdominals and back. Your abdominal muscles comprise four primary muscles that work together to flex your spine, rotate your body, and pull in your abdomen: the rectus abdominus, external oblique, internal oblique, and transverse abdominus. The rectus abdominus works to pull your upper body toward your lower body when you sit up from a lying down position, as you would do in a crunch exercise. The obliques are responsible for bending your spine to the side, rotating your spine, and tilting your pelvis. Found in the deepest layer of the abdominal muscles, the transverse abdominus functions as a natural corset, enveloping your lower abdomen to support your spine and internal organs.

The main core muscles in the back are the multifidus and the erector spinae group. The mul-tifidus muscles are the deepest muscles of the lower back. They connect the spinal vertebrae and are crucial in bending your back. When these muscles are underdeveloped, lower back pain can result. The erector spinae is made up of three layers of muscle that run along the entire length of both sides of your spinal column from the base of your skull to the sacrum, a large, triangular bone at the base of the spine and at the upper and back part of the pelvic cavity. The erector spinae muscles help you maintain an erect posture and keep your spine stable and mobile. The core exercises in the Biggest Loser fitness program are designed to work all of these muscles, give you greater strength and stability, and produce a tighter, more toned midsection.

When Fat around the Middle Is a Health Risk

Having excess fat around your waistline can be hazardous to your health. Why? Abdominal fat cells are quite adept at accommodating fat if you eat more calories than you burn off. As more fat is stored in your belly, your waist widens inch by inch. Most of this fat is packed away in the deep fat layers of your abdomen. Unlike a lot of fat tissue, deep abdominal fat is metabolically active, meaning that it easily disperses fatty acids into the bloodstream. These fatty acids head directly to the liver and into your circulation. With a glut of fat,

Five Healthy Habits for a Super-Sculpted Core

1. **Stop smoking.** Smoking is not a good way to stay thin, contrary to popular belief. In fact, research shows that smokers tend to be fat around the waist. Scientists believe that smoking wreaks havoc on your hormonal systems, which in turn causes fat to be distributed around the midsection.

2. **Curtail alcohol.** Excessive alcohol consumption (more than 1 or 2 drinks a day) has been shown to elevate levels of the hormone cortisol, a stress hormone that is linked with the storage of abdominal fat.

3. **Eat more fiber-rich foods.** A Harvard study found that when men added just 12 grams of fiber to their daily diet, their waistlines decreased by a quarter of an inch. High-fiber foods include beans and legumes, whole grain cereals, fruits, and vegetables.

4. **Add some soy to your diet.** Researchers at the University of Alabama found that postmenopausal women who took a daily supplement of soy protein dropped inches from their abdominal area over a period of 3 months.

5. **Make the Biggest Loser fitness program and the Biggest Loser diet a permanent part of your lifestyle.** Research shows that women, in particular, who repeatedly go on and off diets tend to carry more abdominal fat than those who keep their weight fairly stable.

muscle cells become resistant to the hormone insulin—which means insulin can't do its job of bringing glucose (blood sugar) inside cells for nourishment and the body loses its ability to regulate glucose. This condition is termed *insulin resistance*, and it can lead to type 2 diabetes. People with insulin resistance tend to have high blood pressure, high triglycerides (blood fats), and less HDL cholesterol (the beneficial kind), and are thus at risk for heart disease. Luckily, decreasing abdominal fat lowers your risk of insulin resistance and its associated diseases. You can do this by following a nutritious, calorie-controlled diet such as the Biggest Loser diet; maintaining a healthy weight; and exercising, including exercises that target the abdominals.

The Core Exercises
for the Biggest Loser Fitness Program

Core exercises are vital. Begin with the basic version of each exercise. When you feel stronger and more confident in your body's ability to progress, take the next step to the advanced version of the exercise. Do not try to progress too rapidly. Correctly performed movements are more effective than sloppy ones. It is mastery of exercise form that counts most.

Most of the time, you should be in the "neutral position" when performing core work. This means that your spine is in its natural S-shaped position, with three normal curves: one in your neck, one in your upper back, and one in your lower back. Keeping a neutral spine places the least stress on your muscles and joints because you are balancing the tension in all your muscles to stabilize your position.

Some additional tips include:

- Read through each of the exercise descriptions carefully; note the correct exercise technique as demonstrated by the trainer in the photographs.
- If your core is a "trouble spot" for you, and you desire a trimmer, more taut midsection, start walking. In a number of studies, walking has been shown to preferentially reduce abdominal fat.
- Don't neglect diet for a tight, toned waistline, either. Cutting fatty foods from your daily diet can help zap tummy fat. In one study, when a group of 124 women reduced dietary fat, they each lost 10 to 15 pounds, and more than half the women lost body fat mostly from their abdomen.
- There's no need to do hundreds of reps of core exercises every day. Following the core exercise guidelines here will put you on the path toward lean, fat-free abs and a strong back.

Crunches

Many of us have weak abdominals and lower backs—two muscle groups that are important when performing any type of daily activity. Crunches strengthen and tone these muscles.

Positioning

Lie on your back on an exercise mat or carpeted surface with your feet planted firmly on the surface. Cross your arms over your chest.

The Move

Using the strength of your abdominal muscles, lift your upper torso off the floor toward your thighs. This movement should be very short. Don't attempt to actually touch your thighs, as this can overstress your lower back. Keep constant tension on your abdominal muscles throughout the exercise. With a controlled motion, return to the starting position, and repeat the exercise for the suggested number of repetitions.

Advanced Tips

There are two ways you can make this exercise more advanced. One is to use weights for extra firming action. Follow the instructions above, only hold a weight plate or light dumbbell in front of your chest for extra resistance as you perform the Crunch.

The other advanced exercise is to perform your Crunches on a stability ball. Using a ball forces your abdominals to work harder just to stabilize you atop the ball. Lie back on the stability ball so that it supports your lower back. Keep your knees bent and your feet flat on the floor. As you do in the regular Crunch, cross your arms over your chest and slowly raise your shoulders to no more than a 45-degree angle from the horizontal. Hold, then lower slowly. Continue for the suggested number of repetitions. You can make this version even more challenging by moving your feet closer together.

Oblique Crunches

Here's an excellent waist trimmer that's a great addition to your abdominal work. It isolates the side-waist muscle group called the *obliques* and when included as a part of abdominal exercises, ensures a total workout for the waist.

Positioning

Lie on your left side on an exercise mat or carpeted floor. Bend your knees and curl slightly at the hips. Clasp your hands behind your neck.

The Move

Raise yourself up slightly by lifting your upper torso off the floor, contracting your waist. Return to the starting position and continue the exercise for the suggested number of repetitions. Repeat the exercise on the other side of your body. Keep your core engaged throughout the entire exercise.

Advanced Tip

As you master this move, try to increase the number of repetitions you can do each time you exercise. Abdominal muscles benefit from numerous repetitions.

Jim Germanakos's Exercise Tip

Do not interlock your fingers while doing crunches. It will strain your neck.

Bicycle Maneuver

This exercise is one of the best abdominal exercises science has to offer. The proof: A study conducted at the Biomechanics Lab at San Diego State University compared 13 different exercises that target the midsection, ranging from the Crunch to exercises that employed at-home and gym equipment. According to the findings, the top-ranked exercise was the Bicycle Maneuver, an exercise that has been around for a long time and is a staple of exercise classes everywhere. Compared to exercises like the Crunch (which is a great waist-firming move), the Bicycle Maneuver was 2½ times more effective at working the obliques, and at least 50 percent better at strengthening the rectus abdominus, the main ab muscle that runs the length of your torso.

Positioning

Lie on your back on an exercise mat or carpeted surface. Keep your lower back pressed into the surface and flatten the arch of your lower back; place your fingers on the side of your head just behind your ears. Bend your knees so that your thighs are at about a 90-degree angle to the floor.

The Move

Simultaneously, lift your shoulders off the floor and bring your left knee to your right armpit, while straightening your right leg. Using a slow bicycle-pedaling motion, straighten your left leg, while bringing your right knee in toward your left armpit. Extend your legs out only as far as is comfortable for you, without arching your back. Continue alternating in this fashion for the suggested number of repetitions.

Advanced Tip

Unlike other muscles, you can work your abdominals every day. With the bicycle maneuver, try to work up to five or six sessions a week for a more advanced abdominal workout.

Captain's Chair

Ranking right up there with the Bicycle Maneuver for ab-tightening power is the Captain's Chair, which takes its name from a type of chair having a low back with spindles that curve forward. All you need is a sturdy, armless chair to do this move.

Positioning

Sit up straight on a weight bench and grip the sides of the bench to stabilize your upper body.

The Move

Slowly draw your knees up toward your chest. Hold for a moment, then lower slowly. Repeat the move for the recommended number of repetitions. Keep the motion of raising and lowering your legs very controlled. Concentrate on using the strength of your abdominal muscles to push through the exercise, or else you could place too much stress on your lower back.

Advanced Tip

Rather than grip the sides of the bench, hold your arms out to the sides at shoulder length to perform the exercise. Another way to make this exercise more challenging is to attach ankle weights to your ankles for additional resistance.

Vertical Leg Crunches

This is an alternate version of the basic Crunch—one that will help you achieve a flat, toned stomach, as long as you stick with a healthy diet and regular aerobic exercise.

Positioning

Lie on your back on an exercise mat or carpeted surface. Extend both legs straight up in the air so that they are perpendicular to the floor. Place your hands lightly behind your neck. Keep your core tight and engaged.

The Move

Slowly raise your head, shoulders, and upper back off the floor—no more than 3 to 5 inches. To protect your neck, be careful to not use your arms to pull your neck up. Hold for a moment, then return to the starting position. Repeat for the suggested number of repetitions.

Advanced Tip

An advanced version of this exercise uses a medicine ball. Lie face-up with your knees bent. Hold a medicine ball in both hands outstretched above your chest. Pull your abs up and in without jutting out your rib cage, keeping a neutral spine. Lift your head, neck, and shoulder blades off the floor, using the strength of your ab muscles. Hold for a moment at the top of the exercise. Then reverse the path, curling back down toward the floor.

Phil Hawk's Exercise Tip

Control your breathing; breathe in through your nose and out through your mouth.

Reverse Crunches

This version of the popular Crunch places special emphasis on tightening your lower abdominals. This ensures that you work your midsection from a variety of angles for added core strength and stability.

Positioning

Lie on an exercise mat or carpeted surface with your arms at your sides and feet off the floor. Bend your knees at 90 degrees. Slowly, flex your abs and press your back into the floor, flattening your arch.

The Move

Lift your hips 2 to 4 inches off the floor. Hold for a moment, then lower slowly. Repeat the move for the suggested number of repetitions.

Advanced Tip

To make this move more challenging and build greater core strength, use a stability ball. Lie on your back on a mat or carpeted floor and hold a stability ball between your legs. Raise your legs up off the floor (at about a 90-degree angle). Proceed to curl your hips up 2 to 4 inches off the floor towards your shoulders. Return to the starting position of 90 degrees and repeat.

Half Roll-Ups

This exercise is effective for building core stability, enhancing posture, and flattening your abs. Master the Half Roll-Up before progressing to the advanced Full Roll-Up.

Positioning

Lie on your back on an exercise mat or carpeted surface, with your legs stretched out and your arms at your sides, palms facing down. Press your ab muscles into the floor, flattening your arch.

The Move

Lift your shoulders and upper torso off the floor, forming a "C" shape—about half way up. Your head should come up last. Slowly return to the starting position, following the same path, with your head touching the floor last. Repeat the roll-up for the suggested number of repetitions.

Advanced Tip

As your core becomes stronger, aim to master the Full Roll-Up. Lift your head, then your upper body, forming a "C" shape, until you are sitting up, with your arms stretched out in front of you. Drop your head and upper body forward onto your legs, with your arms stretched forward over your legs to touch your toes. Experience a nice stretch in your spine. Using the same path, roll back down to the starting position, vertebra by vertebra, lengthening your body on the floor. Repeat the roll-up for the suggested number of repetitions.

Plank

The Plank is another exercise that has scored high on the list of effective core exercises. With the proper technique, this basic core exercise develops your abdominals, stabilizes your spine, and strengthens your back.

Positioning

Lie face down on an exercise mat or carpeted surface. Rest on your forearms with your palms flat on the floor. Keep your spine in the neutral position.

The Move

Push off the floor, so that your body is parallel to the floor, and raise up on your toes. Rest on your elbows. Keep your back flat and your body in neutral alignment from your head to your heels. Think of your body as a table being supported by two sets of "legs" (your arms and feet). Hold this position for as long as you can, up to 60 seconds. Repeat for the suggested number of repetitions.

Advanced Tip

While in the plank position, try taking one leg off the floor. This makes your abdominal muscles work harder to keep the body from tilting to the side of the unsupported leg.

Amber Walker's Exercise Tip

Always keep your core tight.

Side Plank

The Side Plank is a variation of the Plank and helps strengthen your obliques, the side-lying muscles of your core.

Positioning

Lie on your side on an exercise mat or carpeted surface.

The Move

Raise your body off the ground and balance yourself with your forearm and the side of your bottom foot. Rest your other arm at your side. Make sure your body forms a straight line from head to heels. Contract your abdominals. Hold this position as long as you can, up to 60 seconds. Repeat for the suggested number of repetitions. Repeat on the other side.

Advanced Tip

An advanced version of this exercise is to balance yourself with your supporting arm fully extended and your other arm outstretched toward the ceiling, making both arms one straight line.

Isabeau Miller's Exercise Tip

If you don't break a sweat, you aren't working hard enough.

Back Extensions

A vital part of developing core stability is to strengthen the lower back. This simple exercise is amazingly effective for doing so. If you have any lower back pain, however, talk to your physician before doing this exercise, or any other move that targets the back.

Positioning

Lie on your stomach on an exercise mat or carpeted surface. Rest your arms at your sides.

The Move

Gently contract your lower back muscles and lift your chest 3 to 5 inches off the floor. Don't strain; just raise your chest as much as you can. Hold for a moment, then slowly lower. Repeat the move for the suggested number of repetitions.

Advanced Tip

For a more challenging version of this exercise, place your hands under your chin or extend your arms straight out in front of you (like a superhero) to do the move. Keep your neck in the neutral position.

Hollie Self's Exercise Tip

Keep going, even when you think you can't, because you can.

Hip Extensions

One of the core's most important jobs is to hold our bodies upright, despite the poor-posture abuse we give them. This simple yet challenging move can help you retrain and strengthen your abdominals and back so that you'll stand taller and look more fit.

Positioning

Kneel on an exercise mat or carpeted surface and place your hands on the mat, under your shoulders, about shoulder-width apart. Keep your spine in neutral alignment.

The Move

Slowly lift an opposite arm and leg up together. Pause, then return to the starting position. Repeat with the other arm and leg. Alternate in this fashion for the suggested number of repetitions.

Advanced Tip

Try to gradually increase the number of repetitions you perform in order to make this exercise more challenging.

TRAINER TIP:
JILLIAN MICHAELS

If you're a woman, you cannot bulk up by lifting weights. This is a huge myth! As women, we don't really have enough testosterone for this to occur. In fact, quite the opposite is true. We should lift weights in order to help us build as much muscle as possible to rev up our metabolism and maintain our bone density.

Wood Chops

From the moment you get out of bed in the morning to the time you retire at night, you perform many movements that involve rotation—swiveling in your desk chair at work, climbing in and out of your car, turning to look at something, or picking up your children. The following exercise is a functional rotation movement designed to help you better perform these basic patterns of daily living and guard against inflexibility and possible injury. Developing a strong rotational component to your body is essential for maintaining everyday fitness. You'll need a dumbbell or a medicine ball to perform this exercise.

Positioning

Stand with your feet shoulder-width apart and hold a dumbbell or medicine ball with both hands.

The Move

Bend at your waist and hold the weight at your right side. Keeping your hips forward, sweep your arms up and across your body in a diagonal until your arms are over the left side of your body. As you perform this move, make sure you're lifting from your core to produce the rotational movement. Repeat this movement for the recommended number of repetitions. Then repeat the move the other way.

Advanced Tip

You can progressively increase the challenge of this exercise by using a heavier medicine ball or weight as you become stronger.

Bob's and Kim's Tips for Flatter Abs and a Stronger Core

- **Get off balance.** Anytime you're on an unstable surface (like using a stability ball or Xerdisc)—and therefore trying to balance—you're developing your core strength. I once had my team pull in their guts and stand on one leg while doing bicep curls to help tone their middles.—Bob Harper

- **Suck it in.** Very motivated contestants like Adrian Kortesmaki from Season Three wanted to work on their abs even when they weren't working out! One trick: Constantly pull your stomach in to work your transverse abdominus, the deepest layer of muscle in your core. This also improves your posture, so your stomach looks even flatter.—Kim Lyons

- **Sit and sculpt.** Sit on a stability ball instead of a chair to work your abs all day long. It's a wonderful way to engage your muscles without having to think about it.—Bob Harper

- **Crunch and twist.** Regular crunches are great, especially if you can lift your feet off the ground and make a 90-degree twist from side to side. I recommend 3 sets of 20—more if you can.—Kim Lyons

- **Ride on.** Do up to 10 minutes of bicycle pedaling in the air while you are lying on your back to work your abdominals.—Bob Harper

- **Work your back.** Many people forget that back strength helps support your abs. So do some back extensions on a stability ball. I suggest doing as many back extensions as you can do regular crunches.—Kim Lyons

What to Expect

You'll see slenderizing results in your waistline early on from this workout. That's because abdominal fat tends to be preferentially reduced in response to aerobic-type exercise, circuit training included. When you exercise aerobically, as you'll do in the Biggest Loser fitness program, you'll start melting fat from your midsection fairly quickly. Since you'll be doing plenty of core work, your abdominal muscles will become developed while you're shedding the fat that overlays them. The result is a total program to help you achieve your best core and abs ever.

5

A Strong and Lean Lower Body

How about a show of hands: How many of you wish you had a better-looking lower body? Probably most of you who raised your hands are women who want trim hips and lean and shapely legs. For many women, thighs and buttocks are considered "problem areas," since fat tends to naturally deposit there. Luckily, the exercises you'll do for your lower body will help you "spot-tighten" these areas and get greater definition and muscle tone. What's more, the aerobic effect created by circuit training helps you burn fat throughout your entire body, including your thighs and buttocks.

Biggest Loser trainer Bob Harper cautions women to not get overly focused on fixing "flawed" body parts. "Whenever I start working with women, I hear complaints like 'My thighs are too big' or 'What can I do about my butt?'" he says. "Once you get someone moving, however, that can change to, 'Wow, I

never knew how weak I was.' Being aware of a flaw can be good for getting you started, but it's more productive to think about being fit and healthy than about how you look."

Guys, there are many of you out there who want more powerful, defined legs too. The exercises in this chapter will help you add mass and muscularity where you didn't have it before, plus build a foundation of power in your legs.

Aesthetics aside, lower-body training has an important functional element too. By working this area of your body, you're preparing yourself for daily living. With strong, stable legs, you can lift kids or heavy boxes, keep your balance while standing on a train, and participate successfully in sports. There's also the matter of injury prevention. Case in point: The knees are one of the most injury-prone joints since they carry much of the body's weight. One of the best ways to protect your knees is to strengthen your quadriceps (thigh) muscles through resistance training exercises.

Targeted Muscles

The exercises detailed here focus on the muscles on the front of the upper leg, collectively known as the quadriceps; the muscles on the back of the upper leg, the hamstrings; the abductors, the outer-thigh muscles; the adductors, the inner thigh muscles; the calf muscles of the lower leg; and of course, the gluteal, or buttock, muscles. Each move works several muscle groups at once, making the exercises not only time efficient, but also ideal for building functional strength in your lower body.

What Really Fights Cellulite?

Cellulite is not a disease or medical problem, but rather a recognized cosmetic condition related to the underlying structure of the skin. It is basically fat tissue just under the skin that results in a lax, dimpled skin surface covering the thighs, buttocks, and hips. Though most prevalent in women, men have cellulite, too. Here are proven strategies for minimizing this condition:

- Lose weight gradually to preserve your skin's suppleness.

- Don't crash diet; it makes cellulite worse by reducing the skin's elasticity.

- Employ targeted muscle development with exercises like squats and lunges to smooth out underlying flabby muscles.

- Do at least 200 minutes a week of pure aerobic exercise, such as walking, in order to burn fat.

- Promote the resilience of your skin by not smoking, avoiding excessive sun exposure, and getting plenty of antioxidants from fruits and vegetables.

What to Expect

The moves described here are huge calorie blasters because they call into action many large muscle groups. When added to a fast-paced circuit routine (see Chapter 7), you'll maximize the calorie burn. The payoff is well worth it, as you watch your lower body change and become noticeably leaner in a month or two.

TRAINER TIP:
JILLIAN MICHAELS

You can reduce the appearance of cellulite by losing weight and building up the muscles underneath your fat tissue. Some good exercises for this are squats and lunges. Ninety-five percent of women suffer from cellulite, including me. Honestly, at some point we have to embrace our imperfections. They make us human. Who wants perfect? Perfect is boring!

The Lower-Body Exercises
for the Biggest Loser Fitness Program

No matter what condition your lower body is in, the Biggest Loser trainers have selected the "best of the best" exercises. If you have bony chicken legs, these exercises will help you build firm muscle for quality size. If you are bottom-heavy, these exercises will give you more shape and definition. If you're happy with your legs and hips, these exercises are the solution to keeping them that way.

Now, a few safety tips and reminders before you start:

- Read through each of the exercise descriptions carefully; note the correct exercise technique as demonstrated by the trainer in the photographs.
- When performing any lower body exercise, such as a squat or lunge, your knees shouldn't travel beyond your toes.
- On any exercise incorporating resistance bands, make sure the bands are free from signs of wear, including cracks or worn endings, and that the resistance feels smooth and flexible in use.
- You're working large areas of muscle so concentrate on proper form. Proper form involves slow, controlled motion, without letting the gravitational momentum pull the weight or resistance down too fast; moving the resistance through its full range of motion; and practicing good posture.
- Focus on the muscle you're working. If you don't feel it being activated, this means that you may need change your grip, your body alignment, or the amount of resistance you're using.

Lunges

The Lunge is unique in its ability to work the quadriceps, hamstrings, and buttocks, and thus is an excellent all-around exercise for the lower body. Lunges also enhance your ability to run, jump, and lift, making them an excellent functional exercise. In addition to stimulating muscular development, Lunges also help you build agility and balance. You can do Lunges practically anywhere—home, hotel room, backyard, or gym—making them among the most convenient, versatile exercises ever.

Positioning

Stand with your feet together, toes pointing ahead. Keep your back straight and your arms at your sides.

The Move

Step forward on your right leg as far as possible and bend your right knee until your right thigh is parallel to the floor. From this point, step back to the starting position. Continue the exercise with the right leg for the suggested number of repetitions, then repeat the exercise with the left leg. As you lunge, your front shinbone should be fixed perpendicular to the floor to keep additional pressure off of your knee.

Advanced Tip

You can make this exercise more challenging by adding weight to the movement. Hold a dumbbell in each hand at your sides and perform the lunge movement as described above.

Phil Hawk's Exercise Tip

Tuck your stomach in when you're doing Lunges.

Squats

The Squat is one of the best exercises to develop and define the front of the thigh, as well as the gluteal and hamstring muscles. Like the Lunge, this exercise can be done just about anywhere.

Positioning

Stand with your legs a comfortable distance apart and your arms crossed over your chest. Keep your back straight.

The Move

Bend at your knees, squatting down until your thighs are just beyond parallel to the floor. Press up from your heels and return to the starting position. Repeat the exercise for the suggested number of repetitions. Concentrate on letting your thighs do all the work.

To protect your lower back, be sure to maintain the neutral alignment in your spine—namely a normal, slightly arched, curvature. If your spine rounds, the risk of injury to the discs greatly increases. When you maintain a normal curvature, your spine can better withstand the resistance in a very safe manner. Similarly, maintain a proper head alignment by keeping your vision focused forward. If you look down, you may round your spine, making that area of the spine weak and more susceptible to injury and loss of stability.

Advanced Tip

You can make this exercise more challenging by adding weight to the movement. Hold a dumbbell in each hand at your sides and perform the squat movement as described above.

Ryan Rodriguez's
Exercise Tip

When squatting, keep your toes in front of your knees.

Thigh Adductions

This exercise targets the inner thigh (the adductors), an important area to work. Strong adductor muscles help stabilize your legs and knees and help prevent injuries that are common when you squat or lunge. They also contribute to overall balanced muscle usage of the entire thigh, and this can help you avert lower-body aches and pains. Working your adductors builds functional strength and performance for movements like kicking a soccer ball, horseback riding, dancing, and any other sort of activity that involves a lot of inner thigh strength. For this exercise, you'll need exercise tubing.

Positioning

Secure one end of a length of exercise tubing around an immovable object and the other end around your right ankle. Make sure you form a loose loop around your ankle so you don't cut off your circulation. Stand erect with your left leg planted firmly on the floor. Hold on to a stable object or press your hand against the wall for balance and support.

The Move

Keep your left knee slightly bent and your hips square. Sweep your right leg across your body and directly in front of your left leg. Pause a moment and then carefully return to the start. Complete the exercise set for the suggested number of repetitions, then repeat with the other leg.

Advanced Tip

When you're ready for more resistance and more challenge, shorten the tubing or use a thicker piece of tubing.

Plie Squats

With this version of the Squat, you activate more of your inner thighs (adductors) than with a regular squat. This exercise, which you may recognize as a ballet move, is the perfect companion to Squats and Lunges for rounding out your lower body routine.

Positioning

Stand with your feet slightly farther apart than hip-width, with your toes and knees turned out comfortably and aligned with each other. Keep your back straight.

The Move

Bend your knees, lowering your hips without rotating your pelvis forward or backward, into a squat. Keep your abs contracted. Straighten your legs and repeat for the suggested number of repetitions.

Advanced Tip

You may add weight to this exercise for an advanced challenge. Either hold a dumbbell in each hand and place them on your upper thighs, or hold a single dumbbell or barbell plate with one hand in front of your body. Perform the exercise as directed above, using proper form.

Isabeau Miller's Exercise Tip

For a variation on Squats, hold a medicine ball to work both your upper and lower body.

Wall Squats with Stability Ball

An effective—and fun—way to perform Squats is to use a stability ball. This variation not only works your thighs and buttocks, it also gives your core a good workout because it requires you to contract your ab muscles while performing the move. The stability ball also provides back support during the exercise.

Positioning

Stand with your back toward a wall and place the stability ball so that it is pressed between your lower back and the wall. Your feet should be placed about shoulder-width apart, with your weight on your heels as if you were about to sit on a chair. Keep your back pressed into the ball for support.

The Move

Bend your knees, keeping your core muscles tight. Lower your body so that your thighs are just parallel to the floor. Keeping your back pressed into the ball, return to the starting position. Repeat the exercise for the recommended number of repetitions.

Advanced Tip

As your thighs become stronger, decrease your pressure against the ball. This will increase the challenge to your lower body muscles.

Static Wall Squats

This exercise perfects and strengthens your thigh muscles and takes only minutes to perform. It looks easy, but you'll really feel it work your legs. No equipment is required except for a wall, making it a perfect exercise for when you are traveling.

Positioning

Stand with your back against the wall and place your feet about shoulder-width apart. Keep your weight on your heels as if you were about to sit on a chair. Keep your back pressed into the wall for support.

The Move

Bend your knees, keeping your core muscles tight. Lower your body so that your thighs are just parallel to the floor. Keep your back pressed into the wall. Hold this position for as long as you can, up to 1 minute. Rest, then repeat.

Advanced Tip

Work on increasing the time you can maintain the squat position. Try this exercise with a partner and see who can hold the position the longest!

Side Lunges

The Side Lunge works the muscles of your inner thigh (adductors), with secondary emphasis on your front thighs.

Positioning

Begin with your feet together, your back straight, and your arms at your sides.

The Move

Step sideways 2 to 3 feet into a lunge, keeping your other (outstretched) leg as straight as you can. Bend your stepping leg and sit back slightly on your hips until your knee is bent about 90 degrees, or as far as feels comfortable. Press back up with your stepping leg and return to the starting position. Complete the recommended number of repetitions, then repeat the exercise with your other leg.

Advanced Tip

You can perform this exercise with two dumbbells to make it more challenging. As you lunge on your right leg, hold the right dumbbell slightly behind you, and the left one slightly in front of you. Do the opposite as you lunge on your left leg.

Julie Hadden's Exercise Tip

When doing a Side Lunge, make sure your feet stay flat on the ground.

Side Steps

Side Steps work your outer thighs (abductors). You'll need an exercise tube and a large area to move around.

Positioning

Place the exercise tube under your feet and grasp each handle with the opposite hand. Stand straight and keep your core muscles tight.

The Move

Take a large step to the right, keeping tension on the tube and lowering into a squat. Bring your left leg toward your right leg, but without letting up on the tension. Keep stepping toward the right in this fashion for 15 to 20 repetitions, or for the length of the room. Switch sides and step to the left.

Advanced Tip

Put more resistance into this exercise by looping the tube around your hands to make the tube tighter.

Calf Raises

Calf muscles respond well to training, taking shape in as little as 2 months. Developing these muscles gives proportion to your lower legs and power for many sports and activities.

Positioning

Stand on a stair, step, or other slightly raised platform. Hold on to a railing or other structure for balance. Place the balls of your feet on the stair or step so that your heels are just off the step. Bend your knees slightly.

The Move

Raise and lower your feet, getting a good stretch at the bottom of the movement. Do as many repetitions as you can.

Advanced Tips

There are two ways you can change up this exercise to make it more challenging. One is to perform a Single-Leg Calf Raise by wrapping your ankle around the leg you're exercising. This puts more weight on the exercising muscle. The other is to hold a dumbbell in one hand while performing Calf Raises or Single-Leg Calf Raises.

Step-Ups

Like stair-climbing, this exercise targets your buttocks, thighs, and calves and can be aerobic. Consider doing it to music to liven the action and make it more fun.

Positioning

Stand facing a bench or step (a stair step works well). Keep your back straight and your core muscles tight.

The Move

Step up with your right foot, then your left. Then step down with your right foot, followed by the left. Repeat. After 1 minute, switch the lead leg.

Advanced Tip

Hold a dumbbell in each hand while stepping to make this exercise more challenging.

Reverse Lunges with Leg Lifts

This exercise is a solid move for strengthening and toning the gluteal muscles of your buttocks. Do these often enough, and your glutes should become harder and more lifted.

Positioning

Stand with your feet about shoulder-width apart, and your hands on your hips.

The Move

Lunge back with your right leg as far as you can, bending your left knee about 90 degrees. Make sure your left knee doesn't track over your toes. As soon as you lower into the lunge position, contract your gluteal muscles. Then push through and up with your right leg, bringing it forward into a knee raise. Do not arch your lower back during this movement. Hold for a count or two, then return that leg to the starting position. Repeat, alternating legs for the suggested number of repetitions.

Advanced Tip

For a greater challenge, hold a dumbbell in each hand, with your arms extended by your sides, and complete the exercise as described above.

Kai Hibbard's Exercise Tip

Learn to love Lunges and Squats. I do tons of both. They're the no-excuses moves you can do anywhere, even if you're stuck in an elevator.

Bridge Pose with Stability Ball

This is another effective exercise for tightening, strengthening, and lifting your buttocks. You'll need a stability ball for the move.

Positioning

Lie face up on an exercise mat or carpeted surface. Place your arms alongside your body or spread out. Position your feet on the top of the stability ball. Keep your abs contracted to hold your torso stable.

The Move

Lift your hips upward as you press down with your ankles and heels on top of the stability ball. Raise your hips off the floor until your body forms a straight line from your shoulders to your heels. Squeeze your buttocks together and hold for a moment. Release and lower your hips back to the starting position. Repeat for the suggested number of repetitions. You should feel this exercise in your buttocks and in the back of your upper thighs (hamstrings).

Advanced Tip

For more of a challenge, try this exercise with only one leg placed on the ball and the other leg crossed over it at the knees. Switch legs and repeat the exercise.

6

Cooling Down

These could be an exerciser's favorite words: "It's time for the cooldown!" They signal the often-welcome end of your exercise session, in which you slow your pace with some light activity. Many people are unaware of the importance of the cooldown, or they tend to skip out on it before their workout is over. But honestly, it is just as important as the warmup—but important for different reasons. While the warmup prepares your body and mind for exercise, the cooldown has an altogether different purpose.

During exercise, your body undergoes some necessary, but taxing, changes. Muscle and connective tissue are microscopically damaged, and waste products such as lactic acid build up in your body. Your lungs work harder, and your heart rate increases to deliver oxygen to the working muscles. Muscles use up energy faster than the bloodstream can supply it. After exercising, it is imperative to restore your body to its pre-exercise state, and you can do this with a *cooldown*.

The cooldown keeps blood circulating to help flush out metabolic wastes and deliver oxygen and nutrients required by muscles, ligaments, and tendons for repair. It also prevents the pooling of blood in your extremities (which can cause fainting), reduces muscle soreness, and helps your heart rate return to normal. It takes anywhere from 5 to 10 minutes to cool down, but check your pulse to be sure. You know you've reached the proper post-workout state if your heart rate falls to, or below, 100 beats a minute.

What is the best way to cool down? We recommend a series of light stretches using a basic technique called *static stretching,* which involves holding a stretch position between 15 and 30 seconds. Like all forms of stretching, static stretching has the power of restoration, relaxation, and rejuvenation when performed properly. Omitting it will diminish the effectiveness of your workout. Plus, stretching is one of the most underrated ways to get lean and trim. Part of the uniqueness of stretching is that it lengthens your muscles, and you begin to look leaner as a result.

Another reason you'll look more trim has to do with your posture. Strong and flexible muscles—achieved through stretching—keep your joints aligned and are the building blocks of good posture. In fact, one of the quickest ways to look slim is to stand up straight. It's true. Employ great posture and you look thinner in minutes. Good posture, in turn, promotes joint health. There's more: Longer muscles let you exert a greater force around a joint, which gives you greater power, which in turn helps you lift more weight, or run or walk faster. Your workouts become more productive, meaning they'll produce results more rapidly.

Cooling Down Is Important

There are many other important reasons for stretching. It will do the following.

Promote Flexibility

Reaching for a jar on a high shelf, bending over to tie your shoes, balancing a kid on one hip, or look-

Kae Whang's Exercise Tip

Breathe! Don't hold your breath; try keeping a steady flow. It will help you stay calm and not hyperventilate.

ing over your shoulder to check oncoming traffic—these are examples of everyday activities that require you to be *flexible*. Flexibility describes being able to move a joint or muscle through its entire range of motion (path) without stiffness, limitation, or pain. Regular stretching is the primary way to increase your range of motion. With greater flexibility and range of motion, you'll be able to generate more force for a more productive workout—which leads to greater muscle tone and definition. Once achieved and maintained, flexibility is instrumental in preventing injuries and muscle soreness, supporting good posture and alignment, and enhancing youthful agility.

Strengthen Your Muscles

Any amount of stretching that you add to your cooldown will also help strengthen your muscles and improve your exercise performance. Research shows that stretching after a workout that involves resistance can increase strength gains by up to 20

How Flexible Are You? Take Kim Lyons's Flexibility Self-Test

Are you flexible as elastic or stiff as a board? Take Kim's test to find out. The test:

Stand with your feet flat on the floor, about 6 inches apart. Bend at your waist and try to touch your toes, but without bending your knees. Reach your arms down as far as you can toward your toes. Here's how you rate in terms of flexibility:

- Palms of your hands flat on the floor in front of your feet: Excellent

- Hands to your feet: Good

- Hands to your ankles: Fair

- Hands to your knees: Poor

Regardless of your score, the good news is that you can improve your flexibility through regular stretching, or by taking classes in yoga or Pilates. Flexibility improves quickly, so take this test from time to time, and you'll feel good about the progress you're making.

percent. Although it is not clear why, scientists speculate that stretching may increase a muscle's responsiveness, making it more receptive to the stimulus of the resistance. So stretch—you'll feel stronger. Don't consider it a choice.

Release Tension

Stretching has important psychological and stress-relieving benefits, and thus is a wonderful escape valve. So many of us hold tension in our shoulders, neck, back, hamstrings, chest, and other areas, mostly caused by the physical and mental stresses we encounter. We spend countless hours sitting in front of our computers or hunched over our desks, or we're running through our day at a frantic pace that is a threat to our bodies and minds.

Every muscle in your body houses *stretch receptors*, which communicate with your brain about the level of muscular tension. When your muscles are chronically tight, your body suffers from misalignment, creating poor posture and shortened, constantly contracted muscles. That notifies your brain you're under stress or experiencing tension. Just as chronically tight muscles send a signal to your brain that you're tense and stressed out, chronically relaxed muscles send the opposite message, telling your brain that everything is okay. That can make you feel less stressed out even when you're laboring under a ton of pressure.

So with regular stretching, you release locked-up tension and your body instinctively responds in a positive, relaxed mode. Biggest Loser trainer Bob Harper is a big believer in regular stretching and feels that this response may even help you if you're an emotional eater—someone who reaches for food when something stressful happens. "It's my job to help stop that behavior," says Bob. "Creating better habits like stretching—with its psychological benefits—can make stress a little more manageable." As you stretch, use your mind's eye to visualize the body you want to achieve.

Rejuvenate Your Body

As you get older, your muscles tend to stiffen and become less flexible. There's less of that spring and range of motion you had in your youth. Your joints aren't moving at full capacity. Fluids that lubricate your muscles and joints also tend to dry up. So what can you do? First of all, take the attitude that it's never too late to postpone these effects of aging and improve your flexibility at the same time. Second, start a program of regular stretching. It is a wonderful antidote and gives you a sense of control over age-related changes in your body. There is no physiological reason that a healthy person in his or her later years cannot walk tall, move with confidence, and feel young. If you're stiff and feel weak, it is generally because of inactivity, not your age. There is no good reason to say "no" to stretching.

Stretching Do's and Don'ts

Stretching is one of the easiest fitness moves you can perform. Before you begin, here are some do's and don'ts to keep in mind as you reach for a longer, more fit, and trim body.

- **Do** stretch as a cooldown. Your whole body is warm; this is the best time to stretch.
- **Do** breathe during your stretches. Oxygen exchange is necessary for your muscles to begin repair and recovery. Inhale as you get into position for the stretch; exhale as you move into it.

By employing full inhalations and full exhalations, you are energizing and revitalizing your system. Holding your breath, on the other hand, could increase your blood pressure.

- **Do** remember that there are two sides to your body. If you stretch one triceps, for example, remember to stretch the other.

- **Do** take time to stretch if you have diabetes. People with diabetes tend to form more *glycosylation end products* in their bodies than people without diabetes. These are created when glucose links up (glycates) with various substances in the body, including cartilage and collagen. This reaction causes these tissues to stiffen and lose flexibility, making you more prone to tendonitis, inflammation, and poor healing. Stretching properly promotes flexibility and reduces the possibility of injury under these conditions.

- **Do** listen to your body. If you feel unusual pain, or a lot of swelling, it's time to see your doctor. You could be dealing with a serious injury, such as a torn ligament or inflammation of tissue.

- **Don't** stretch a "cold" muscle. If you do that, you could tear a muscle instead of gently stretching it. Your muscles need to have some blood pumping through them and be warm and at least somewhat pliable to be stretched safely and effectively.

- **Don't** push your body past the point of comfortable movement or stretch to the point of feeling pain. Fortunately, muscles are outfitted with a safety mechanism called a *stretch reflex*. When you push a muscle too far, this sensor kicks in, and the muscle responds reflexively by contracting. It shortens the muscle to protect it from overextending the joint. Although this response protects the muscle, it prevents you from being able to lengthen tight muscles.

- **Don't** bounce as you stretch. Bouncing increases momentum and can lead to microscopic tears in muscle fibers.

- **Don't** stretch in a hurry. If you try to do it in less time, you run the risk of injury. Use the cooldown as a time to relax not only your muscles, but also your mind.

Cooldown Stretches
for the Biggest Loser Fitness Program

Here are eight cooldown stretches selected by the Biggest Loser trainers. Do these at the conclusion of your workout, and you'll see a huge difference in how your body looks, feels, and responds. Also, these moves are some of the best stress relievers around.

Here are some additional pointers and reminders:

- Read through each of the stretch descriptions carefully; note the correct technique as demonstrated by the trainer in the photographs.
- The cooldown is key! It keeps the body active and prevents pooling of blood in your extremities. The stretches promote increased blood flow to your muscles; increase flexibility and range of motion; and decrease your risk of injury.
- Think you don't have time for meditation? Think again. Use the cooldown not only as a time to bring your body back to norm, but also as a chance to experience inner calm and deep relaxation.
- For an extra treat, do something yoga instructors often employ during cooldowns: Rub a dab of lavender oil on your hands, then massage your neck, as part of your cooldown, and breathe in the gentle scent. There may be something to this technique: In a study conducted at the University of Alaska, a group of men were exposed to lavender aromatherapy following a workout. Their blood pressure and heart rate returned to normal slightly faster than in those who were not given aromatherapy.

Calf Stretch

Stand with your toes at the edge of a stair or low bench. Lower one heel toward the ground until you feel a good stretch in your calf. Hold for 15 to 30 seconds. Repeat with the other leg.

Patty Gonzalez's Exercise Tip

Have fun and enjoy yourself.

Hamstring Stretch

Sit on an exercise mat or carpeted surface with your legs slightly apart. Bend forward from your waist, keeping your knees straight. Try to reach your fingers toward your toes. Hold for 15 to 30 seconds.

Kae Whang's Exercise Tip

Know your limits! It's okay to push yourself farther, but not to a point of injury. Listen to your body. And wear good shoes. Go to an expert or pay that little extra for a comfortable fit. Your back and knees will thank you.

One-Arm Reach-Across

Stand with your feet shoulder-width apart. Lift your left arm up in an arc over your head and tilt your body to the right, getting a good stretch in your obliques at the side of your core. Reach and stretch your left arm as high as you can. Switch sides and stretch with your right arm.

Hip Flexor Stretch

Kneel with your left knee on an exercise mat or carpeted surface and your right knee up. Place your hands on your right knee. Lunge forward slightly on your left knee to get a good stretch in your thigh and hip. Hold for a moment or two, then repeat the stretch on the opposite leg.

Neil Tejwani's Exercise Tip

Don't wear tight clothing while working out.

Triceps Stretch

Place one arm overhead, with your elbow pointing toward the ceiling. Position your forearm close to your upper arm and head. Grasp your elbow with your other hand. Pull your elbow back slightly and toward your head. Hold the stretch for a few seconds and repeat with the other arm.

Quad Stretch

Bend your right knee and bring your right foot toward your back and hold it with your right hand. Hold on to a wall or sturdy table with your left hand, if necessary. Keep your left knee slightly bent. Gently pull up and back on your foot, stretching your thigh. Hold for 15 to 30 seconds. Repeat the stretch with your other leg.

Child's Pose

Kneel down on an exercise mat or carpeted surface and sit back toward your heels, while extending your arms and torso forward. Rest your forehead on the floor. Stretch your back and relax your neck and shoulders. Hold for 15 to 30 seconds.

Heather Hansen's Exercise Tip

I refuse to exercise on Sundays. I believe in giving the body a day to rest. And don't get discouraged. One week I lost only 1 pound and I was just incredibly disappointed. But then I got out the measuring tape and learned I lost 3½ inches overall! That's the power of exercising.

Low Back and Glute Stretch

Lie on your back on an exercise mat or carpeted surface and bend your knees. Clasp your arms and hands around your lower legs and gently pull your knees to your chest until you feel a nice stretch in your lower back. Next, cross your legs, placing one ankle on the opposite knee. Use the flexed leg to press the crossed leg back until you feel a gentle stretch in your buttocks. Repeat this sequence with the other leg.

David Griffin's Exercise Tip

Make sure you get proper rest.

When you know it's time to "cool down," don't dismiss it. Welcome it as a time to unwind, literally and figuratively. Enjoy the freedom of movement. As you stretch, fill your mind with positive thoughts of becoming stronger, more flexible, and more attractive, rather than with self-deprecating thoughts about deficiencies in your body that you're trying to correct. There is nothing you cannot achieve if you put your mind to it, and this is certainly true when you think about your own body. Before long, you'll create the results you are looking for. You are in charge of your fitness destiny.

Jillian Michaels's Nutritional Cooldown

After your workout, certain nutrients in your body are depleted—including glycogen, protein, fluid, and electrolytes—along with protective antioxidants. To restore what's lost, give yourself a *nutritional cooldown*, too. The benefits are numerous: greater energy levels each time you exercise, less fatigue, better muscular development, and stronger immunity so you don't have to miss workouts. Here are some tips for cooling down nutritionally:

- Enjoy a carbohydrate/protein snack following your workout: a bagel with a slice of reduced-fat cheese, a fruit smoothie made with nonfat yogurt, cottage cheese and fruit, or nuts and an apple. Together, protein and carbohydrates trigger the release of insulin and growth hormone in your body. Insulin is a powerful factor in developing muscle, and growth hormone promotes the burning of fat for energy.

- If you don't feel like eating right after your workout, try some liquid nutrition, such as a canned protein/carb beverage or shake.

- Have two 8-ounce glasses of water after your workout to restore fluids.

- For extra insurance, make sure to take a multiple vitamin/mineral supplement each day (one that contains antioxidants).

7

The Biggest Loser Workout

Y ou are about to begin a workout that will reshape your body, push you farther than you've probably ever gone before, and uncover strength and stamina you didn't know you had. All we ask is that you stay with it, one workout at a time, and make devoting yourself to it a top priority. If you can do that, the dedication you put forth will help you change not only your body, but your life, too. You'll discover that you can do anything successfully as long as you put your heart and mind into it.

Here's something we know can help you: Continue to draw inspiration from your favorite Biggest Loser cast members. They pushed beyond their physical limits, broke the psychological bonds that had kept them overweight and unhappy, and made exercise a destined-to-last habit. Take Shannon Mullen from Season Two, for example. What surprised her most was how hard she could actually work out. "Before the show, my idea of exercise was window shopping," Shannon says. "It was never a part of my life. Now I can't get enough."

Another role model is Andrea Overstreet, also from Season Two. She works out 5 days a week—3 days at a 5:00 a.m. boot camp class and 2 days at a yoga class. She designed her life to fit exercising in her schedule, without taking too much time away from her family. Even family time is active: Andrea, her husband, and kids bike or swim for recreation. Thanks to her new healthier eating habits and active lifestyle, Andrea is training for the 2008 Los Angeles Marathon and will be walking in a 39-mile Avon breast cancer walk. She has so fully integrated physical activity into her life that it has become a part of who she is and what she stands for.

The same dramatic changes happened to Pam Smith, the first person to be voted off the ranch in Season Three. In 2007, Pam served as the spokesperson for the INshape Indiana campaign promoted by the governor to get the entire state to lose 10 pounds in 10 weeks. Later in the year, she and her husband competed in a sprint triathlon—something she never would have attempted had she not embraced fitness as a lifestyle. Pam is a true inspiration to others—a fan watched her on television, began a walking program, and lost 82 pounds—so let her and all the other Biggest Loser contestants be an inspiration to you. If you look in the mirror and do not like what you see, don't worry. Those extra pounds, which have been the source of so much unhappiness, are about to become a disappearing act.

Adrian Kortesmaki's Exercise Tip

The first time I went running, I couldn't do more than 2 minutes, so I alternated running, skipping, and walking. Within 2 months, I was running a mile in under 10 minutes.

Getting Started

Starting this workout is one of the most important investments you can make in yourself. You're beginning this journey to get a better body, but guess what? Along the way, you'll discover that becoming fitter pays incredible health dividends. With your physician's approval to exercise, physical activity has enormous benefits in addition to losing weight or shaping up:

1. People who exercise live longer, on average, than people who don't.

2. Active people have a lower risk of dying from heart disease and stroke, and they're less likely to get high blood pressure.

3. The more active you are, the lower your risk of colon cancer.

4. The less active you are, the higher your risk of developing type 2 diabetes. If you already have type 2 diabetes, exercise can lower your blood sugar levels.

5. In people with arthritis, moderate exercise helps reduce joint swelling and pain and improves mobility.

6. Strength-building exercise helps counter bone loss (osteoporosis).

7. Exercise makes you *functionally fit*, meaning that it's easier for you to carry groceries, do chores, and independently perform many other activities of daily life.

8. Because of the calming effect of exercise, active people are less depressed, and depressed people often feel better after they start exercising.

9. Exercise can save you money. If you can prevent serious—and costly—medical conditions such as heart disease, cancer, and osteoporosis, you will have more money for your other needs.

10. Exercise can be fun! Many of the activities you did for play as a child count as exercise. Dancing fast, walking your dog, bicycling, and gardening all strengthen your heart and lungs.

Sound awesome? Then you're all set. Take these steps to get underway:

Step 1: Find Your Fitness Level

When you begin a new fitness program, it is often confusing to determine how much exercise you need to do and how hard you should work out. Don't worry—we'll help you figure it out. What's so empowering about the Biggest Loser fitness program is that it accommodates all levels of fitness and conditioning. Week by week, this progressive program advances with you, affecting positive changes in your appearance, the way you feel, and your health. So that you know exactly where to start the workout, take the assessment

Suzy Preston's Exercise Tip

Find an exercise partner. Bob Harper made me run a few hundred feet, initially. Eventually I got to a mile, but I was not a strong runner. Later, I'd run with Seth, a friend on the men's team. He would push me by saying, "Don't hold on to the treadmill," and I'd say back, "Okay, crank it up then." I still don't love running, but if I'm with somebody else, at least we can have fun.

below to see whether you're a beginner, intermediate, or advanced exerciser. Determining your level will help you do exactly the right amount of exercise—and begin the process of creating a whole new body. So grab a pen or pencil, read through the questions, and check the answers that best describe you.

1. Describe the frequency with which you exercise:
   - A. The last time I exercised was last year, or 6 months ago; or I can't remember the last time I exercised.
   - B. I've been exercising for a couple of months, on average of 3 times a week.

C. I've been exercising regularly for 6 months or longer, several times a week.

2. How much endurance (aerobic) exercise do you do?

   A. I don't do any aerobic exercise.

   B. I exercise aerobically 30 to 90 minutes a week.

   C. I exercise aerobically more than 90 minutes a week.

3. How much strength training do you do?

   A. I've never done any strength training.

   B. I have done some strength training, but only sporadically.

   C. I've been strength training regularly for 3 months or longer.

4. How would you rate your flexibility?

   A. I don't think I'm very flexible since I rarely stretch.

   B. I occasionally stretch, but it's not something I do regularly.

   C. I make it a habit to stretch and/or I regularly attend yoga or Pilates classes.

5. What benefits have you experienced from exercising?

   A. I don't think I've exercised enough, or consistently, in the past to get results.

   B. When I do exercise, I know I feel better, and I know it's good for me.

C. Exercise has helped me lose weight and/or control my weight, feel more energetic, and feel better about myself.

Scoring: Look back over your answers. If you answered mostly A to the questions, you're at the beginner level; mostly B, the intermediate level; and mostly C, the advanced level. Here are key guidelines for each level.

Jerry Lisenby's Exercise Tip

Proper form is a must! Keep your feet planted to the floor at all times. Each rep should be done properly and slowly.

Beginner Level

- Beginners will perform a circuit routine only once per session. This means you'll do one set of each exercise and immediately move to the next exercise with only 5 to 8 seconds between exercises.
- After 2 weeks, you will begin performing a circuit twice. This means you'll do one set of each

exercise, immediately move on to the next, and so forth, until you've performed all the exercises in sequence. Then you'll start over, thus completing two circuits.

- When you feel stronger on a particular exercise or want more challenge, try the advanced version of the exercise in question.

Intermediate Level

- Intermediate exercisers will perform a circuit routine twice. For example, do one set of each exercise, immediately move on to the next, and so forth, until you've performed all the exercises in sequence. Then you'll start over, thus completing two circuits.
- After 2 weeks, or when you feel stronger, perform a circuit three times.
- When you feel stronger on a particular exercise or want more challenge, try the advanced version of the exercise in question.

Advanced Level

- Advanced exercisers will perform a circuit three times.
- Opt for the advanced version of each exercise when you work out. Sometimes even the most advanced exercisers hit a plateau and don't experience the progress they want. The routines,

with their advanced exercises, will kick your program up and help you make new fitness breakthroughs. Give it all you've got, step up to the plate, and really push through it. In the end, you'll take your fitness—and your body—to a whole new super-fit level.

Nicole Michalik's Exercise Tip

Bring music! It keeps you going, especially high tempo music, and always listen to Bob!

Step 2: Assemble Your Equipment

You'll want to wear sturdy, well-fitting athletic shoes and clothing that breathes and allows you to move freely. Wear a heart rate monitor and have a watch with a second hand so that you keep your rest periods between sets short. The basic exercise equipment you'll need includes pairs of dumbbells that increase incrementally in weight; resistance tubing; a stability ball; and ankle weights. Optional is an Xerdisc. If you want to save money, consider buying used equipment, as long as it is in good shape. For dumbbells, you can get creative by filling milk jugs with water or sand, or using heavy books as weights.

Step 3: Select from One of Three Routines

So that you won't stagnate or ever get bored, we've supplied three different circuit training workouts. You can do one for a month, switch to another the next month, then try the third workout in your third month. This versatility in workouts is great for breaking plateaus. Kim Lyons advises: "A plateau means your body is getting used to the exercise you've been doing, so shake up your routine by changing it. Doing so can reignite weight loss."

With three workouts, this program will vary what you've been doing in the past, plus give you extra challenges, so that you remain excited about it forever!

Step 4: Start Moving

Now you're ready to start moving. Some tips to help you:

- If possible, exercise in front of a mirror to track and maintain proper alignment and form.
- Stay present in the moment when you are lifting a weight or doing an exercise, and connect to your body. Be in touch with your breathing and aware of how your body feels.
- All levels—beginner, intermediate, and advanced—should gradually progress to heavier resistances. This maximizes the EPOC effect— the length of time your metabolic rate stays elevated following your exercise routine. Norwegian scientists found that the heavier the training, the longer and stronger the rise in metabolic rate after the workout. In their study, subjects who lifted heavy weights experienced an increase of 18 percent in metabolic rate 1 day after their workout and 11 percent 2 days afterward, compared to those who lifted lighter weights (an increase of 13 percent the next day, and 4 percent 2 days later). So to drop the most fat in the least amount of time, strive to use heavier weights when you train.
- Listen to your body signals. Pain, dizziness, shortness of breath, or nausea are signals that you should stop and take a break. You may be pushing yourself too hard.
- Be sure to warm up and cool down properly. This workout can be more intense than traditional training because of its simultaneous demands on the upper and lower body, as well as the cardiovascular system. The warmup and cooldown prepare your body for these demands.
- When performing an exercise, choose a weight or resistance that allows you to perform only the specified range of repetitions. If the exercise is too easy, progressively increase the weights or try the advanced version of the exercise.

Biggest Loser Fitness
Circuit Training Routines

Remember, our fitness plan is based on the concept of circuit training, in which you perform one set of each exercise for 1 minute, or usually 10 to 12 repetitions, then immediately advance to the next exercise with only 5 to 8 seconds of rest in between. You'll be on the move constantly, and this boosts the intensity of the workout. The rapid transition from one exercise to next really burns fat and works your heart and lungs hard for improved cardiovascular fitness. After a warmup, you'll work your upper body first, your core muscles next, and your lower body last. You'll end your routine with a series of relaxing stretches for your cooldown. You should be able to complete the circuit in about 30 minutes (longer if you're at the advanced level), moving through the circuit once, twice, or three times, depending on your level of conditioning. Circuit training is an ideal way to train if you have limited time during the day.

Keep in mind the many other benefits of this style of exercising: It provides an effective stimulus to create enough muscle tone and development over your entire body, it keeps your metabolism charged up, and it provides a host of health benefits, from an improved mood to a strengthened immune system. Of course, you'll not only lose weight, but inches too.

Perform your circuit routine three times per week, resting at least a day between workouts.

Routine #1: Beginner

The Warmup

Step Touches:
1 minute
(page 24)

Arm Raises:
1 minute
(page 25)

Simulated Jump Rope: 1 minute
(page 26)

Shoulder Rolls:
Forward 10 to
15 seconds;
backward 10 to
15 seconds
(page 27)

Neck Rolls:
30 seconds
(page 28)

Marching in Place: Up to 5 minutes
(page 29)

Upper Body Exercises

Biceps Curls:
1 set, 10 to
12 reps
(page 35)

Triceps Dips:
1 set, 10 to
12 reps
(page 37)

Dead Lifts:
1 set, 10 to 12
reps
(page 45)

Chest Flies:
1 set, 10 to
12 reps
(page 40)

Shoulder Presses: 1 set,
10 to 12 reps
(page 43)

Overhead Pullovers: 1 set,
10 to 12 reps
(page 44)

Core Exercises

Crunches: 1 set,
10 to 12 reps
(page 53)

Oblique Crunches:
1 set, 10 to
12 reps
(page 54)

Captain's Chair:
1 set, 10 to
12 reps
(page 56)

Plank: Hold
60 seconds,
repeat 2 or 3 times
(page 60)

Back Extensions:
1 set, 5 to 8 reps
(page 62)

Lower-Body Exercises

Lunges: 1 set,
10 to 12 reps
(page 71)

Thigh Adductions:
1 set, 10 to
12 reps
(page 73)

Step-Ups: 1 set
of 1 minute,
each side
(page 80)

**Reverse Lunges
with Leg Lifts:**
1 set, 10 to 12 reps
(page 81)

Calf Raises: 1 set,
up to 25 reps
(page 79)

The Cooldown

Calf Stretch: Hold 15 to 30 seconds each leg
(page 91)

Hamstring Stretch: Hold 15 to 30 seconds
(page 92)

One-Arm Reach-Across: Hold 15 to 30 seconds each side
(page 93)

Hip Flexor Stretch: Hold 15 to 30 seconds each side
(page 94)

Triceps Stretch: Hold 15 to 30 seconds each side
(page 95)

Quad Stretch: Hold 15 to 30 seconds each side
(page 96)

Child's Pose: Hold 15 to 30 seconds
(page 97)

Low Back and Glute Stretch: Hold 15 to 30 seconds each side
(page 98)

Routine #1: Intermediate

The Warmup

Step Touches:
1 minute
(page 24)

Arm Raises:
1 minute
(page 25)

Simulated Jump Rope: 1 minute
(page 26)

Shoulder Rolls:
Forward 10 to
15 seconds;
backward 10 to
15 seconds
(page 27)

Neck Rolls:
30 seconds
(page 28)

Marching in Place: Up to
5 minutes
(page 29)

Upper-Body Exercises

Perform each exercise for one set, then repeat the entire routine for a second set.

Biceps Curls:
2 sets, 10 to 12
reps each
(page 35)

Triceps Dips:
2 sets, 10 to
12 reps each
(page 37)

Dead Lifts:
2 sets, 10 to
12 reps each
(page 45)

Chest Flies:
2 sets, 10 to
12 reps each
(page 40)

Shoulder Presses: 2 sets,
10 to 12 reps
each *(page 43)*

Overhead Pullovers:
2 sets, 10 to
12 reps each
(page 44)

Core Exercises

Perform each exercise for one set, then repeat the entire routine for a second set.

Crunches: 2 sets,
10 to 12 reps each
(page 53)

Oblique Crunches:
2 sets, 10 to 12
reps each
(page 54)

Captain's Chair:
2 sets, 10 to 12
reps each
(page 56)

Plank: Hold 60
seconds, repeat
2 or 3 times
(page 60)

Back Extensions:
1 set, 5 to
8 reps each
(page 62)

Lower-Body Exercises

Perform each exercise for one set, then repeat the entire routine for a second set.

Lunges: 2 sets,
10 to 12 reps each
(page 71)

Thigh Adductions:
2 sets, 10 to 12
reps each
(page 73)

Step-Ups: 2 sets of
1 minute each,
each side
(page 80)

**Reverse Lunges with
Leg Lifts:** 2 sets,
10 to 12 reps each
(page 81)

Calf Raises: 2 sets,
up to 25 reps each
(page 79)

The Cooldown

Calf Stretch: Hold 15 to 30 seconds each leg
(page 91)

Hamstring Stretch: Hold 15 to 30 seconds
(page 92)

One-Arm Reach-Across: Hold 15 to 30 seconds each side
(page 93)

Hip Flexor Stretch: Hold 15 to 30 seconds each side
(page 94)

Triceps Stretch: Hold 15 to 30 seconds each side
(page 95)

Quad Stretch: Hold 15 to 30 seconds each side
(page 96)

Child's Pose: Hold 15 to 30 seconds
(page 97)

Low Back and Glute Stretch: Hold 15 to 30 seconds each side
(page 98)

Routine #1: Advanced

The Warmup

Step Touches: 1 minute *(page 24)*

Arm Raises: 1 minute *(page 25)*

Simulated Jump Rope: 1 minute *(page 26)*

Shoulder Rolls: Forward 10 to 15 seconds; backward 10 to 15 seconds *(page 27)*

Neck Rolls: 30 seconds *(page 28)*

Marching in Place: Up to 5 minutes *(page 29)*

Upper-Body Exercises

Perform each exercise for one set, then repeat the entire routine for the second and third sets.

Biceps Curls: 3 sets, 10 to 12 reps each, seated on a stability ball *(page 35)*

Triceps Dips: 3 sets, 10 to 12 reps each, using a weight placed on your lap *(page 37)*

Dead Lifts: 3 sets, 10 to 12 reps each *(page 45)*

Chest Flies: 3 sets, 10 to 12 reps each, on a stability ball *(page 40)*

Shoulder Presses: 3 sets, 10 to 12 reps each *(page 43)*

Overhead Pullovers: 3 sets, 10 to 12 reps each *(page 44)*

Core Exercises

Perform each exercise for one set, then repeat the entire routine for the second and third sets.

Crunches: 3 sets, 10 to 12 reps each, with extra weight or on stability ball
(page 53)

Oblique Crunches: 3 sets, 10 to 12 reps each
(page 54)

Captain's Chair: 3 sets, 10 to 12 reps each, with ankle weights or holding your arms out to your sides
(page 56)

Plank: Hold 60 seconds, repeat 2 to 3 times, lifting one leg off the floor
(page 60)

Back Extensions: 1 set, 5 to 8 reps, with your hands under your chin or extending your arms straight out in front
(page 62)

Lower-Body Exercises

Perform each exercise for one set, then repeat the entire routine for the second and third sets.

Lunges: 3 sets, 10 to 12 reps each, holding dumbbells at your sides
(page 71)

Thigh Adductions: 3 sets, 10 to 12 reps each, shortening the tubing or using thicker tubing
(page 73)

Step-Ups: 3 sets of 1 minute each, each side
(page 80)

Reverse Lunges with Leg Lifts: 3 sets, 10 to 12 reps each, holding dumbbells at your sides
(page 81)

Calf Raises: 3 sets, up to 25 reps each, holding a dumbbell or doing Single Leg Calf Raises with the free leg wrapped around the exercising leg
(page 79)

The Cooldown

Calf Stretch: Hold 15 to 30 seconds each leg
(page 91)

Hamstring Stretch: Hold 15 to 30 seconds
(page 92)

One-Arm Reach-Across: Hold 15 to 30 seconds each side
(page 93)

Hip Flexor Stretch: Hold 15 to 30 seconds each side
(page 94)

Triceps Stretch: Hold 15 to 30 seconds each side
(page 95)

Quad Stretch: Hold 15 to 30 seconds each side
(page 96)

Child's Pose: Hold 15 to 30 seconds
(page 97)

Low Back and Glute Stretch: Hold 15 to 30 seconds each side
(page 98)

Routine #2: Beginner

The Warmup

Step Touches:
1 minute
(page 24)

Arm Raises:
1 minute
(page 25)

Simulated Jump Rope: 1 minute
(page 26)

Shoulder Rolls: Forward 10 to 15 seconds; backward 10 to 15 seconds
(page 27)

Neck Rolls: 30 seconds
(page 28)

Marching in Place: Up to 5 minutes
(page 29)

Upper-Body Exercises

Hammer Curls:
1 set, 10 to 12 reps
(page 36)

Triceps Kickbacks: 1 set, 10 to 12 reps
(page 38)

Dead Lifts: 1 set, 10 to 12 reps
(page 45)

Chest Presses:
1 set, 10 to 12 reps
(page 41)

T-Raises:
1 set, 10 to 12 reps
(page 42)

Bent-Over Row: 1 set, 10 to 12 reps each side
(page 46)

Core Exercises

Bicycle Maneuver:
1 set, 10 to 12 reps
(page 55)

Half Roll-Ups:
1 set, 5 to 8 reps
(page 59)

Vertical Leg Crunches: 1 set,
10 to 12 reps
(page 57)

Side Plank: Hold
60 seconds, repeat
2 or 3 times
each side
(page 61)

Hip Extensions:
1 set, 5 to 8 reps
each arm and leg
(page 63)

Routine #2: Intermediate

The Warmup

Step Touches:
1 minute
(page 24)

Arm Raises:
1 minute
(page 25)

**Simulated Jump
Rope: 1 minute**
(page 26)

Shoulder Rolls:
Forward 10 to
15 seconds;
backward 10 to
15 seconds
(page 27)

Neck Rolls:
30 seconds
(page 28)

**Marching in
Place: Up to
5 minutes**
(page 29)

Upper-Body Exercises

Perform each exercise for one set, then repeat the entire routine for a second set.

Hammer Curls:
2 sets, 10 to
12 reps each
(page 36)

**Triceps
Kickbacks:**
2 sets, 10 to
12 reps each
(page 38)

Dead Lifts:
2 sets, 10 to
12 reps each
(page 45)

Chest Presses:
2 sets, 10 to
12 reps each
(page 41)

**T-Raises: 2 sets,
10 to 12 reps
each**
(page 42)

Bent-Over Row:
2 sets, 10 to
12 reps each
side
(page 46)

Core Exercises

Perform each exercise for one set, then repeat the entire routine for a second set.

Bicycle Maneuver:
2 sets, 10 to
12 reps each
(page 55)

Half Roll-Ups: 1 set,
5 to 8 reps
(page 59)

Vertical Leg
Crunches: 2 sets,
10 to 12 reps each
(page 57)

Side Plank: Hold
60 seconds, repeat
2 or 3 times
each side
(page 61)

Hip Extensions:
1 set, 8 to 10 reps
each arm and leg
(page 63)

Lower-Body Exercises

Perform each exercise for one set, then repeat the entire routine for a second set.

Squats: 2 sets,
10 to 12 reps each
(page 72)

Plie Squats: 2 sets,
10 to 12 reps each
(page 74)

Static Wall Squats:
2 times, hold up to
1 minute
(page 76)

Reverse Lunges with
Leg Lifts: 2 sets,
10 to 12 reps each
(page 81)

Calf Raises: 2 sets,
up to 25 reps each
(page 79)

The Cooldown

Calf Stretch: Hold
15 to 30 seconds
each leg
(page 91)

Hamstring Stretch:
Hold 15 to
30 seconds
(page 92)

**One-Arm
Reach-Across:** Hold
15 to 30 seconds
each side
(page 93)

Hip Flexor Stretch:
Hold 15 to 30
seconds each side
(page 94)

Triceps Stretch: Hold
15 to 30 seconds
each side
(page 95)

Quad Stretch: Hold
15 to 30 seconds
each side
(page 96)

Child's Pose:
Hold 15 to
30 seconds
(page 97)

**Low Back and Glute
Stretch:** Hold 15 to
30 seconds
each side
(page 98)

Routine # 2: Advanced

The Warmup

Step Touches:
1 minute
(page 24)

Arm Raises:
1 minute
(page 25)

Simulated Jump Rope: 1 minute
(page 26)

Shoulder Rolls:
Forward 10 to 15 seconds;
backward 10 to 15 seconds
(page 27)

Neck Rolls:
30 seconds
(page 28)

Marching in Place: Up to 5 minutes
(page 29)

Upper-Body Exercises

Perform each exercise for one set, then repeat the entire routine for the second and third sets.

Hammer Curls: 3 sets, 10 to 12 reps each, seated on a stability ball
(page 36)

Triceps Kickbacks: 3 sets, 10 to 12 reps each
(page 38)

Dead Lifts: 3 sets, 10 to 12 reps each
(page 45)

Chest Presses: 3 sets, 10 to 12 reps each, on a stability ball
(page 41)

T-Raises: 3 sets, 10 to 12 reps each, standing on an Xerdisc or sitting on a stability ball
(page 42)

Bent-Over Row: 3 sets, 10 to 12 reps each side
(page 46)

Core Exercises

Perform each exercise for one set, then repeat the entire routine for the second and third sets.

Bicycle Maneuver: 3 sets, 10 to 12 reps each
(page 55)

Half Roll-Ups: 1 set, 5 to 8 reps, performing a Full Roll-Up
(page 59)

Vertical Leg Crunches: 3 sets, 10 to 12 reps each, with a medicine ball
(page 57)

Side Plank: Hold 60 seconds, repeat 2 or 3 times, with your supporting arm fully extended and your other arm outstretched toward the ceiling
(page 61)

Hip Extensions: 1 set, 10 to 12 reps each arm and leg
(page 63)

Routine #2: Advanced (continued)

Lower-Body Exercises

Perform each exercise for one set, then repeat the entire routine for the second and third sets.

Squats: 3 sets, 10 to 12 reps each, holding dumbbells at your sides
(page 72)

Plie Squats: 3 sets, 10 to 12 reps each, using weights
(page 74)

Static Wall Squats: 3 times, hold up to 1 minute
(page 76)

Reverse Lunges with Leg Lifts: 3 sets, 10 to 12 reps each, holding dumbbells at your sides
(page 81)

Calf Raises: 3 sets, up to 25 reps each, holding a dumbbell or doing Single Leg Calf Raises with the free leg wrapped around the exercising leg
(page 79)

The Cooldown

Calf Stretch: Hold 15 to 30 seconds each leg
(page 91)

Hamstring Stretch: Hold 15 to 30 seconds
(page 92)

One-Arm Reach-Across: Hold 15 to 30 seconds each side
(page 93)

Hip Flexor Stretch: Hold 15 to 30 seconds each side
(page 94)

Triceps Stretch: Hold 15 to 30 seconds each side
(page 95)

Quad Stretch: Hold 15 to 30 seconds each side
(page 96)

Child's Pose: Hold 15 to 30 seconds
(page 97)

Low Back and Glute Stretch: Hold 15 to 30 seconds each side
(page 98)

Routine #3: Beginner

The Warmup

Step Touches:
1 minute
(page 24)

Arm Raises:
1 minute
(page 25)

Simulated Jump Rope: 1 minute
(page 26)

Shoulder Rolls:
Forward 10 to 15 seconds;
backward 10 to 15 seconds
(page 27)

Neck Rolls:
30 seconds
(page 28)

Marching in Place: Up to 5 minutes
(page 29)

Upper-Body Exercises

Biceps Curls:
1 set, 10 to 12 reps
(page 35)

Triceps Kickbacks: 1 set, 10 to 12 reps
(page 38)

Dead Lifts: 1 set, 10 to 12 reps
(page 45)

Push-Ups: 1 set, 10 to 12 reps
(page 39)

Shoulder Presses: 1 set, 10 to 12 reps
(page 43)

Overhead Pullovers: 1 set, 10 to 12 reps
(page 44)

Core Exercises

Crunches: 1 set,
10 to 12 reps
(page 53)

Reverse Crunches:
1 set, 10 to
12 reps
(page 58)

Half Roll-Ups: 1 set,
5 to 8 reps
(page 59)

Wood Chops: 1 set,
10 to 12 reps
each side
(page 64)

Back Extensions:
1 set, 5 to 8 reps
(page 62)

Lower-Body Exercises

**Wall Squats with
Stability Ball: 1 set,
10 to 12 reps**
(page 75)

**Side Lunges:
1 set, 10 to 12 reps
each side**
(page 77)

**Bridge Pose with
Stability Ball: 1 set,
5 to 8 reps**
(page 82)

**Side Steps: 1 set,
15 to 20 reps
each side**
(page 78)

**Calf Raises: 1 set,
up to 25 reps**
(page 79)

The Cooldown

Calf Stretch: Hold 15 to 30 seconds each leg *(page 91)*

Hamstring Stretch: Hold 15 to 30 seconds *(page 92)*

One-Arm Reach-Across: Hold 15 to 30 seconds each side *(page 93)*

Hip Flexor Stretch: Hold 15 to 30 seconds each side *(page 94)*

Triceps Stretch: Hold 15 to 30 seconds each side *(page 95)*

Quad Stretch: Hold 15 to 30 seconds each side *(page 96)*

Child's Pose: Hold 15 to 30 seconds *(page 97)*

Low Back and Glute Stretch: Hold 15 to 30 seconds each side *(page 98)*

Routine #3: Intermediate

The Warmup

Step Touches:
1 minute
(page 24)

Arm Raises:
1 minute
(page 25)

Simulated Jump Rope: 1 minute
(page 26)

Shoulder Rolls:
Forward 10 to 15 seconds; backward 10 to 15 seconds
(page 27)

Neck Rolls:
30 seconds
(page 28)

Marching in Place: Up to 5 minutes
(page 29)

Upper-Body Exercises

Perform each exercise for one set, then repeat the entire routine for a second set.

Biceps Curls:
2 sets, 10 to 12 reps each
(page 35)

Triceps Kickbacks:
2 sets, 10 to 12 reps each
(page 38)

Dead Lifts:
2 sets, 10 to 12 reps each
(page 45)

Push-Ups:
2 sets, 10 to 12 reps each
(page 39)

Shoulder Presses: 2 sets, 10 to 12 reps each
(page 43)

Overhead Pullovers: 2 sets, 10 to 12 reps each
(page 44)

Core Exercises

Perform each exercise for one set, then repeat the entire routine for a second set.

Crunches: 2 sets,
10 to 12 reps each
(page 53)

Reverse Crunches:
2 sets, 10 to
12 reps each
(page 58)

Half Roll-Ups: 1 set,
5 to 8 reps
(page 59)

Wood Chops: 2 sets,
10 to 12 reps
each side
(page 64)

Back Extensions:
1 set, 5 to 8 reps
(page 62)

Lower-Body Exercises

Perform each exercise for one set, then repeat the entire routine for a second set.

Wall Squats with
Stability Ball: 2 sets,
10 to 12 reps each
(page 75)

Side Lunges: 2 sets,
10 to 12 reps
each side
(page 77)

Bridge Pose with
Stability Ball: 2 sets,
5 to 8 reps each
(page 82)

Side Steps: 2 sets,
15 to 20 reps
each side
(page 78)

Calf Raises: 2 sets,
up to 25 reps each
(page 79)

The Cooldown

Calf Stretch: Hold 15 to 30 seconds each leg
(page 91)

Hamstring Stretch: Hold 15 to 30 seconds
(page 92)

One-Arm Reach-Across: Hold 15 to 30 seconds each side
(page 93)

Hip Flexor Stretch: Hold 15 to 30 seconds each side
(page 94)

Triceps Stretch: Hold 15 to 30 seconds each side
(page 95)

Quad Stretch: Hold 15 to 30 seconds each side
(page 96)

Child's Pose: Hold 15 to 30 seconds
(page 97)

Low Back and Glute Stretch: Hold 15 to 30 seconds each side
(page 98)

Routine #3: Advanced

The Warmup

Step Touches:
1 minute
(page 24)

Arm Raises:
1 minute
(page 25)

Simulated Jump Rope: 1 minute
(page 26)

Shoulder Rolls:
Forward 10 to
15 seconds;
backward 10 to
15 seconds
(page 27)

Neck Rolls:
30 seconds
(page 28)

Marching in Place: Up to
5 minutes
(page 29)

Upper-Body Exercises

Perform each exercise for one set, then repeat the entire routine for the second and third sets.

Biceps Curls:
3 sets, 10 to
12 reps each,
seated on a
stability ball
(page 35)

Triceps Kickbacks:
3 sets,
10 to 12 reps
each
(page 38)

Dead Lifts:
3 sets,
10 to 12 reps
each
(page 45)

Push-Ups:
3 sets, 10 to
12 reps each,
without bending
your knees
(page 39)

Shoulder Presses: 3 sets,
10 to 12 reps
each
(page 43)

Overhead Pullovers:
3 sets,
10 to 12 reps
each
(page 44)

Core Exercises

Perform each exercise for one set, then repeat the entire routine for the second and third sets.

Crunches: 3 sets, 10 to 12 reps each, with extra weight or on stability ball
(page 53)

Reverse Crunches: 3 sets, 10 to 12 reps each, with stability ball
(page 58)

Half Roll-Ups: 1 set, 5 to 8 reps each, performing a Full Roll-Up
(page 59)

Wood Chops: 3 sets, 10 to 12 reps each side, with medicine ball
(page 64)

Back Extensions: 1 set, 5 to 8 reps each, with your hands under your chin or extending your arms straight out in front
(page 62)

Routine #3: Advanced (continued)

Lower-Body Exercises

Perform each exercise for one set, then repeat the entire routine for the second and third sets.

Wall Squats with Stability Ball: 3 sets, 10 to 12 reps each, decreasing pressure against the wall
(page 75)

Side Lunges: 3 sets, 10 to 12 reps each side, holding dumbbells
(page 77)

Bridge Pose with Stability Ball: 2 sets, 5 to 8 reps each, with right leg only placed on stability ball for set 1, and left leg on ball for set 2
(page 82)

Side Steps: 3 sets, 15 to 20 reps each side
(page 78)

Calf Raises: 3 sets, up to 25 reps each, holding a dumbbell or doing Single Leg Calf Raises with the free leg wrapped around the exercising leg
(page 79)

The Cooldown

Calf Stretch: Hold 15 to 30 seconds each leg
(page 91)

Hamstring Stretch: Hold 15 to 30 seconds
(page 92)

One-Arm Reach-Across: Hold 15 to 30 seconds each side
(page 93)

Hip Flexor Stretch: Hold 15 to 30 seconds each side
(page 94)

Triceps Stretch: Hold 15 to 30 seconds each side
(page 95)

Quad Stretch: Hold 15 to 30 seconds each side
(page 96)

Child's Pose: Hold 15 to 30 seconds
(page 97)

Low Back and Glute Stretch: Hold 15 to 30 seconds each side
(page 98)

Adding Cardio

It's fine to add in some pure cardio exercise such as walking or jogging week by week, too—anything that gets your heart rate up and lets you keep it there for at least 20 minutes. This can be as simple as walking around the block in your neighborhood. Trainer Bob Harper says, "Take little steps—something you can easily manage. This will give you a sense of accomplishment that will make you come back for more."

Although our circuit routine is aerobic, you can obtain added fat-burning power with two or three cardio sessions a week. Cardio increases fat-burning enzymes in your body. You need those enzymes if you want to get leaner. Plus, cardio builds your oxygen-processing capacity. Fat is burned only when there's adequate oxygen around.

Be sure to choose an activity you enjoy doing, too, so that you can stick to it. Another consideration is how the aerobic activity stimulates certain parts of your body. For example, if you need better development in your lower body, think about walking, jogging, or even running. All three are lower body activities. Swimming, on the other hand, is an upper body aerobic activity. Or you might mix up your cardio work, doing different types of exercise—a method called *cross training*—to work more of your muscles and give you variety to prevent burnout.

Another tip from the Biggest Loser trainers and contestants: If you do cardio on the same day as circuit, do it *after* your circuit training. This sequence accentuates fat loss. Following your circuit routine, your body is low on stored carbohydrates (glycogen). Consequently, your body will tap into its fat stores to help burn energy.

So consider building some cardio into your schedule. Here is what your weekly workout plan might look like:

Sunday	Rest Day
Monday	Circuit and Optional Cardio
Tuesday	Cardio
Wednesday	Circuit and Optional Cardio
Thursday	Rest Day
Friday	Circuit and Optional Cardio
Saturday	Cardio

Log Your Progress

We like to see you keep track of when you worked out—and how long, and whether you increased your resistances or reps, or progressed to any advanced exercise moves. These are all indicators of progress and help you stay the course.

Also, record milestones such as pounds or inches lost, a new smaller dress or pants size, or your ability to exercise longer without getting tired. There are other not-so-obvious milestones worth recording too, such as:

Improved blood pressure
Better blood sugar control
More energy and mental focus
Better sleep
Lower resting heart rate
Improved cholesterol and triglycerides levels

Basically, you're keeping a record of your success, written down in black and white. Making behavior changes is a challenge, but progress motivates.

Consistency

There will be times when you might have to miss a workout. Just don't get upset over it and let your distress overtake your motivation. Missing a single workout in no way means that you can't stick to an exercise schedule. This would be a self-destructive mind set. Allowing such negativity to intrude in your life might even make you miss a string of workouts, or set you up to fall off your diet. Let it go and focus on doing your next workout, and your next, and so forth. Says Bob Harper: "It doesn't matter how far off track you've gone if you just make a concerted effort every day—the smallest step—you can get control of your life again."

Try taking a lesson from competitive athletes; they do mental warmups. Start thinking about the benefits of your upcoming workout. The calories you burn. The muscle you'll firm. Your body reshaping itself, all in the right places. The stress-relieving chemicals that will flood your system. Imagine how invigorated and rejuvenated you'll feel afterward. See yourself consistently following your schedule one workout at a time. Replay this information in your head. Make a promise to yourself that when you start the Biggest Loser fitness plan, you will be committed to it. Stay with your schedule, and before long, an active lifestyle will become a second-nature habit. Now go for it—you'll be amazed at what you can accomplish today.

TRAINER TIP:
JILLIAN MICHAELS

I advocate 4 hours of resistance training a week. Do cardio as extra credit. The more cardio you do on top of your resistance training, the more rapidly you will lose weight.

8

The Biggest Loser Diet

Now you're ready to tackle another big issue: how to eat to melt those pounds from your body. Surprise: We're not going to suggest that you starve yourself down to size. If you're a regular watcher of *The Biggest Loser,* or a member of the Biggest Loser Club (www.BiggestLoserClub.com), you already know that crash diets are self-defeating.

The Biggest Loser diet—which calls for a moderate reduction in fat and carbs combined with calorie control—should help you burn pound after pound of pure fat—and do so without feelings of deprivation or loss of energy. To boost your fat loss, the diet is high in lean protein, which has a hunger-controlling effect on the body. On this diet, you'll enjoy a healthy new way of eating that will help you manage your weight and feel satisfied while you're doing it. You'll see steady results in no time.

Controlling Calories

Early in season three, the Biggest Loser experts tallied up the calories the contestants ate in just one week. Collectively, they consumed two and a half times the recommended amount for a group of 14 people. It takes 3,500 calories to create a pound of fat, and that many additional calories can translate into a weight gain of 468 pounds!

Clearly, the first thing you need to do is be aware of the calories in the food you eat. Calories are basically the measurement of how much energy a food gives you after you eat it. That energy is used by your body to fuel physical activity, as well as all metabolic processes, from maintaining your heartbeat and growing hair to healing a broken bone and building lean muscle. Calories really do count, and they count big time. If you don't eat fewer calories than you burn off, you won't lose weight. The Biggest Loser diet helps give you a calorie deficit—in reduced food intake and increased physical activity—but without making you feel deprived.

Controlling Carbohydrates

It's true that if there's any nutrient we eat too much of, it's carbohydrates. But your brain only runs on glucose, which is a particular kind of carbohydrate. You need those carbs going to your brain just to continue to regulate your breathing and maintain your heartbeat.

Do not exclude carbohydrates completely from your diet, and be sure to eat on time—every 3 to 4 hours. For healthy carb choices, choose whole-grain breads and pastas, brown rice, and sweet potatoes. In addition, watch your carb portion sizes; this varies with individuals but generally you should have no more than 30 to 45 grams per meal, or about 1 cup of rice or 2 slices of bread.

Controlling Fat

It's a healthy move to limit foods high in saturated fat (animal fats, butter, lard, and tropical oils), as well as *trans fats,* which are man-made fats, created when vegetable oil is hardened. Trans fats are found in margarine and many baked goods and junk foods. Both saturated fats and trans fats can clog your arteries when eaten in excess. While it's true that many people eat too many saturated and trans fats (resulting in weight gain), there are good fats that are required for optimal health. Healthy fats play an important role in helping our body use vitamins such as D, E, A, and K. They're also important for healthy skin and hair. Healthy fat choices include olive oil, canola oil, avocados, flax seeds, and dry roasted nuts such as almonds. Moderation is key and the amount of healthy fats that you need depends on the total number of calories you require for weight loss. On the Biggest Loser diet, you have a 200-calorie budget of extra foods, and this budget can be spent on fats and oils, which average up to 120 calories per tablespoon.

THE 4-3-2-1 BIGGEST LOSER PYRAMID

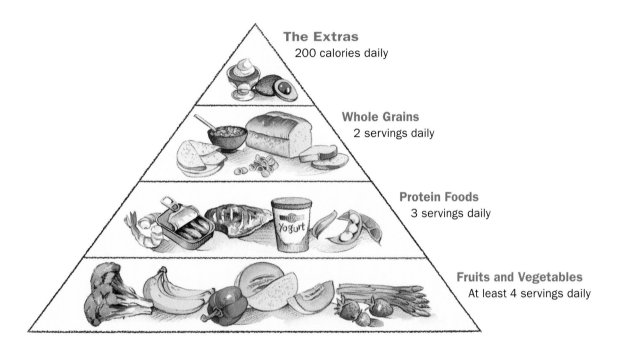

The Extras
200 calories daily

Whole Grains
2 servings daily

Protein Foods
3 servings daily

Fruits and Vegetables
At least 4 servings daily

Planning Your Meals

The 4-3-2-1 Biggest Loser Pyramid

The foods you'll eat are organized into the 4-3-2-1 Biggest Loser Pyramid, which sets out a specific number of servings each day from various food groups. As the illustration shows, this pyramid has fruits and vegetables at its base, protein foods on the second tier, and whole grains on the third tier.

The small section at the tip gives you a 200-calorie budget for any food not included on the lower three tiers.

Each of the food groups represented on the Biggest Loser Pyramid provides most of the nutrients you need daily. Try to center your diet around the foods at the base of the pyramid, and eat fewer servings from the foods toward the top of the pyramid. Let's take a more detailed look at how to plan your meals using the pyramid.

Fruits and Vegetables: 4 Servings Daily, Minimum

At least half of your servings should be from vegetables; the other half from fruits. Don't have more fruit servings than vegetable servings.

Choose these vegetables to lose: Artichoke, asparagus, bamboo shoots, beans (green, yellow), beet greens, beets, broccoli, Brussels sprouts, cabbage, carrots, cauliflower, celery, collard greens, cucumbers, eggplant, kale, kohlrabi, leeks, lettuce (all varieties), mushrooms, mustard greens, okra, onions, palm hearts, parsley, peas, peppers (all varieties), pumpkin, radishes, shallots, spinach, sprouts, summer squash, sweet potatoes, Swiss chard, tomatillos, tomatoes, turnip greens, turnips, water chestnuts, watercress, winter squash, yams, and zucchini

Vegetable serving size: 1 cup or 8 ounces

Choose these fruits to lose: Apple, apricot, banana, blackberries, blueberries, cherries, cranberries, grapefruit, grapes, guava, kiwi, mango, melon (all varieties), nectarine, orange, papaya, peach, pear, persimmons, pineapple, plantain, plums, pomegranate, raspberries, rhubarb, strawberries, and tangerine

Fruit serving size: 1 cup, 1 medium piece, or 8 ounces

Erik Chopin's Diet Tip

A sugar-free fudgsicle makes a great snack and can satisfy any chocolate urge.

You can eat more than 4 servings a day of most fruits and vegetables if you wish. At the base of the pyramid, fruits and vegetables supply the most nutrients in the form of vitamins, minerals, *phytochemicals* (protective plant chemicals), and fiber relative to the low number of calories they contain. In other words, you get the most nutrient bang for your caloric buck from fruits and vegetables.

The exceptions to this are starchy vegetables such as pumpkin, winter squash, corn, peas, white potatoes, sweet potatoes, and yams. These veggies must be eaten in limited portions because of their carbohydrate content. For example, 1 cup of beans (a starchy vegetable) has 15 grams of carbohydrates as opposed to 1 cup of uncooked spinach, a nonstarchy vegetable, which has only 5 grams of carbohydrates.

Starchy vegetables are perfectly fine to eat—just a few servings a week, however. And be sure to watch the portion sizes. Go to town with the nonstarchy veggies such as lettuce, spinach, cucumbers, onions, broccoli, carrots, celery, and beets.

Because they have so few calories, you can consume as many nonstarchy veggies as you'd like.

As for fruits, it's a common misconception that they are so good for us we can eat them in unlimited amounts. Fruit does have good things like vitamins, minerals, and fiber. But fruit is also loaded with sugar, so watch your portion sizes. Make sure that you are eating a minimum of 4 cups of fruits and vegetables each day, and try to eat more vegetables each day than fruits to keep your sugar intake low.

Worth mentioning too: Cut back on dried fruits, including raisins, Craisins, dried cherries, and dried blueberries. Dried fruits are often treated with additives, and they are overly concentrated in calories and fruit sugar, which can play havoc with your blood sugar. Further, they're not as filling as raw fruits, so they do little to help curb hunger. Consider this: Two tablespoons of raisins have as many calories as a whole cupful of grapes. It's much more filling to eat a whole cup of grapes than a little bit of raisins.

Protein Foods: 3 Servings Daily

The Biggest Loser Pyramid recommends three 8-ounce or 1-cup portions of protein foods each day, regardless of your daily caloric limit or target. Here is a closer look at your many protein choices:

Choose these animal proteins to lose: Any type of beef, pork, or veal labeled 95 percent lean; white meat chicken; white meat turkey; egg whites; fish (any type) and shellfish (any type). In selecting fish, try to choose those that are rich in heart-protective fats called *omega-3 fatty acids*. These fish include salmon, sardines (water-packed), herring, mackerel, trout, and tuna.

Animal protein serving size: 1 cup or 8 ounces

Choose these vegetarian proteins to lose: Beans and legumes (black beans, broad beans, chickpeas, edamame, Great Northern beans, kidney beans, lentils, lima beans, navy beans, pinto beans, split peas, white beans, and so forth); miso; soybeans, soy bacon, soy or veggie burgers, soy hot dogs, and other natural (meaning not the powders or pills) soy products; tempeh; and tofu

Vegetarian protein serving size: 1 cup or 8 ounces

Choose these reduced-fat dairy foods to lose: Buttermilk, reduced-fat milk (1%), skim or fat-free milk, soy milk, yogurt (plain), yogurt (no sugar added, fruit flavored), and reduced-fat cottage cheese

Reduced-fat dairy serving size: 1 cup or 8 ounces

Try to include protein at every meal. Here's why: Carbohydrates empty out of your stomach in 20 to 40 minutes. If you eat carbs by themselves, your blood sugar will skyrocket and then plummet.

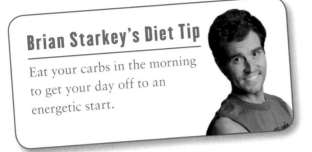

Brian Starkey's Diet Tip

Eat your carbs in the morning to get your day off to an energetic start.

That's what we call the *sugar high and crash*. By contrast, protein takes up to 3 hours to empty out of your stomach. If you eat carbs with protein, those carbs have to empty out of your stomach at the same rate as the protein. As a result, you'll have much more consistent blood sugar levels and increased energy throughout the day. So for breakfast, don't just grab a bagel—which is mostly carbs—and go. Be sure to pair that bagel up with an egg, lox, or cottage cheese.

You can divide your protein up into any size portions you want through the day. For example, you can have half a portion at breakfast, lunch, dinner, and for snacks, as long as you fulfill your protein allotment for the day. Protein is best eaten in smaller quantities, anyway, so your body can use it throughout the day. So make sure you have some protein at each meal.

Protein and Calories

Protein foods vary widely in calories, so making the right protein choice for your caloric needs is important. Below are guidelines that will let you select protein foods consistent with your caloric target.

Lower calorie targets (1,050 to 1,400 calories): This is an appropriate caloric range if you're a woman and exercising at least three times a week, or if you've hit a plateau and need to downshift your calories for a week or two in order to start losing again. In this range, you'll need to select reduced-fat dairy as a protein source most frequently, because it is low in calories, and because the calcium in dairy foods is especially important for bone health in people with lower caloric needs. The Biggest Loser diet thus recommends 2 servings of reduced-fat dairy proteins daily. Your third serving should come from animal protein, vegetarian protein, or a combination of the two.

Midrange calorie targets (1,400 to 1,800 calories): This is a good range for men or women who are exercising several times a week for an hour each time. In this range, the Biggest Loser diet recommends 1 to 2 servings of reduced-fat dairy daily. Your remaining protein servings should come from animal protein, vegetarian protein, or a combination of the two.

Higher calorie targets (1,800 to 2,100 calories): This is good caloric range for men who are exercising several times a week for an hour each time, or for anyone who has achieved his or her weight loss and can increase calories while staying active on a regular exercise program. Aim for at least 1 serving of dairy each day. Protein sources other than dairy should be used to reach your allotment of 3 protein servings daily.

Whole Grains: 2 Servings Daily

The Biggest Loser Pyramid recommends 2 daily servings of whole grains and whole grain products.

Choose these bread products to lose: Whole-grain bread, high-fiber bread (choose brands with around 45 calories per slice), Ezekiel 4:9 breads; Wasa breads; whole-wheat buns, whole-wheat pitas, whole-wheat tortillas, and whole-wheat dinner rolls

Bread serving size: 2 slices (bread), preferably "light;" 1 piece (whole-grain bun or roll); 2 light Wasa flatbreads; 1 whole-wheat flour tortilla

Choose these whole grains to lose: Barley, brown rice, bulgur, corn grits, couscous, cream of rice, cream of wheat, millet, oat bran, quinoa, rolled oats, whole-wheat cereal, whole-wheat pasta, and wild rice

Whole grain serving size: 1 cup cooked

For maximum nutrition, always lean towards the most nutritious grains—those that have undergone the least processing, such as those listed above. Brown rice, for example, is higher in vitamins and fiber than white rice. That's because white rice has been stripped of its husk, germ, and bran layers during processing. Similarly, rolled oats are more nutritious than instant oats. When grains are put through the process of refinement, the important nutrients are taken out. All that's usually left is the starchy interior, which is loaded with carbohydrates and not much else.

Most packaged ready-to-eat breakfast cereals tend to be highly processed and loaded with added sugar. Some exceptions are low-carb cereals (a favorite among cast members) and high-fiber cereals such as Kashi GoLean, Fiber One, Quaker Weight Control Instant Oatmeal, and All-Bran. Packaged cereals containing 5 grams or more fiber per serving are generally considered to be high-fiber cereals.

Another factor to consider when choosing a breakfast cereal is its sugar content. Although all cereals will naturally have some sugar in them, you want to avoid cereals that have a great deal of added sugar. Read the label for sugar content. A good rule of thumb that's easy to remember is to choose packaged cereals with less than 5 grams of sugars and at least 5 grams of fiber per serving.

Tip of the Pyramid: The Extras, Your 200-Calorie Budget

You're given 200 extra calories a day in addition to what you eat from the foods above. Spend your budget on healthy choices and don't squander it on nutritionally bankrupt foods such as candy and sweets. Sensible, healthy choices include the following foods and condiments:

Fats, Oils, and Spreads

- Good fats such as olive oil, canola oil, flaxseed oil, and walnut oil
- Reduced-fat peanut butter and other nut butters

Reduced-Fat Foods

- Cheese, reduced-fat or fat-free
- Sour cream, reduced-fat

Condiments and Sauces

- Broth and bouillon, reduced-sodium
- Barbecue sauce, low-calorie
- Ketchup, low-calorie
- Cocktail sauce
- Chili sauce
- Horseradish
- Mustard
- Picante sauce
- Salsa
- Soy sauce, light
- Steak sauce
- Tabasco sauce
- Tomato paste
- Tomato sauce

- Worcestershire sauce
- Artificial sweeteners, in moderation

Alcohol

- 12-ounce regular beer (about 150 calories)
- 5-ounce glass of wine (about 100 calories)
- 1½-ounce shot of 80-proof distilled spirits (about 100 calories)

Other

- Avocado
- Nuts and seeds
- Pickles (unsweetened)
- Olives

When to Adjust Your Calories

As you bid farewell to those pounds and inches, your calorie requirement will drop. For every 1 pound of fat you lose, you decrease the number of calories you expend each day by about 10. That's roughly the number of calories that were required to keep that fat at body temperature, move it around, and support its metabolic needs. So when you shed 10 pounds of fat, you will be burning up about 100 fewer calories each day than you did when you weighed more. If you want to keep losing weight, you either have to eat fewer calories, exercise more, or do both. Unless you readjust your calories or your exercise, you'll reach equilibrium, or you may even start to gain weight. And that's not an option!

When it's time for you to reduce your calories, there are four easy, near-automatic ways to do so:

1. Cut your calories from your optional 200-calorie budget.
2. Replace your whole-grain servings with vegetables.
3. Choose lower-calorie protein foods such as reduced-fat dairy, egg whites, and soy.
4. Reduce your fruit servings in favor of more vegetables.

Just don't get discouraged! It's highly unlikely that your weight will climb on this plan because the Biggest Loser diet keeps your calories, carbs, and fat in check.

Meal Timing

If you go too long without eating, you'll probably be pretty hungry at your next meal. When you're famished from a long day of not eating, it's quite difficult to not overeat when you do sit down to eat again. This is one of the reasons that we recommend that you eat every 3 to 4 hours on a schedule that includes three main meals (breakfast, lunch, and dinner) and one to three snacks. If your schedule is unpredictable, try to keep healthy snacks like cut vegetables and fruit with you so that you can snack between meals.

How to Structure Your Meals

Okay, now that you understand the basics of the Biggest Loser diet, let's talk about how to put your meals together. What follows is a template to help you create and structure your own meals. You don't have to follow this template exactly. Flexible and adaptable to your needs and tastes, it simply gives you a blueprint for planning your meals and arranging all your servings throughout the course of a day. For example, you don't have to have fruit at breakfast; you might save it for a snack or another meal later. This template can be enormously helpful because it takes all the guesswork out of meal planning and is a breeze to follow.

Julie Hadden's Diet Tip

Keep hydrated at all times. Buy a calorie counter, and weigh your food.

Breakfast

½ protein serving

1 whole-grain serving

1 fruit serving

Snack

½ protein serving

1 fruit serving

Lunch

1 protein serving

½ whole-grain serving

1 vegetable serving

Snack

½ protein serving

1 fruit serving

Dinner

½ protein serving

½ whole-grain serving

2 vegetable servings

Extra

200 calories from additional foods, healthy fats, and condiments

If you adapted the template with allowable foods from the Biggest Loser diet food lists above, your menu—with recipes—for one day might like look something like this:

TRAINER TIP:
JILLIAN MICHAELS

In order to help change your body composition: Avoid sodium whenever possible; it will make your body hold water and feel puffy. Drink 80 ounces of water a day to flush out excess fluids you might be retaining. Cut all refined sugar, processed grains, canned foods, and frozen foods. And, mix up your exercise regimen.

Sample One-Day Menu

BREAKFAST	½ bagel, oat bran (3-inch diameter) Mozzarella cheese, part skim, 1 ounce Orange juice, ½ cup
SNACK	Kelly Minner's Cream Cheese Roll-Ups (page 159), 1 serving Orange, 1 small (2⅜-inch diameter)
LUNCH	Cheese crackers, ½ ounce Icy Gazpacho with Fresh Lime (page 160), ⅓ serving Raisins, 1 miniature box (½ ounce) Yogurt, fruit, ½ cup
SNACK	Cauliflower, raw, 1 cup *Milk chocolate candy, 2 miniature bars
DINNER	*Kraft Light Done Right Ranch Salad Dressing, 2 tablespoons Romaine lettuce (salad), shredded, 2 cups Suzy Preston's Ranch-Style "Spaghetti" Marinara (page 161), ½ serving Turkey, ground, 93 percent lean, 2½ ounces
SNACK	Cantaloupe, diced, 1 cup Dana DeSilvio's Yogurt Parfait (page 162), ½ serving

*These foods count as part of the 200-calorie budget.

Recipes

Every season, Biggest Loser contestants are charged not only with shedding excess pounds, but also with concocting their own get-lean meals in the ranch kitchen. That's where contestants are taught to turn their favorite recipes into dishes that taste great and fight fat at the same time. You can do it, too. First, start by looking for those fattening ingredients in a recipe that make it high in fat or sugar. Second, make substitutions to replace those ingredients (the chart below can help you) or reduce the amount the fattening ingredient to make the recipe healthier. Finally, change your method of preparing food. For example, instead of frying, try grilling, steaming, broiling, baking, or poaching. The recipes that follow, and those in *The Biggest Loser Cookbook*, illustrate just how easy it is to cook up great meals for a great-looking body.

In place of:	Try:
1 cup cheese	1 cup fat-free or reduced-fat cheese
1 cup shortening, margarine, or butter	1 cup unsweetened applesauce or fruit puree; or ½ cup margarine or butter substitute appropriate for baking or pan-frying (check labels)
1 cup sour cream	1 cup fat-free or light sour cream; 1 cup fat-free yogurt; or buttermilk
1 cup heavy cream	1 cup evaporated milk
1 cup milk	1 cup fat-free or 1% milk
1 tablespoon regular mayonnaise	1 tablespoon light or fat-free mayonnaise
1 tablespoon cream cheese	1 tablespoon fat-free cream cheese
High-fat meats, including luncheon meats	Reduced-fat or fat-free meats
Sugar	Sugar substitutes suitable for cooking (check labels); or use half sugar and half sugar substitute; or use unsweetened applesauce, mashed bananas, or other fruits in recipes and cut down on the sugar.
1 cup all-purpose flour	¾ cup all-purpose flour + ¼ cup bran
Pasta and noodles	Spaghetti squash

KELLY MINNER'S CREAM CHEESE ROLL-UPS

Kelly says, "This is a great snack to make when you need something simple but satisfying. You can also make them ahead so they're good-to-go when you need a nibble in a hurry. I prefer the low-fat Lebanese bologna."

- 2 slices roast turkey or turkey bologna (2 ounces)
- 2 tablespoons fat-free cream cheese with chives (or garden vegetable flavor)

Place the turkey slices on a flat surface and spread thinly with the cream cheese. Roll tightly. Cover and refrigerate until serving.

Makes 2 servings

Per serving: 73 calories, 5 g protein, 2 g carbohydrates, 5 g fat (1 g saturated), 22 mg cholesterol, less than 1 g fiber, 434 mg sodium

Jennifer Eisenbarth's Diet Tip

Start and end every meal with a glass of water. If you're too full at the end of the meal to drink the water, you know that you've eaten too much.

ICY GAZPACHO WITH FRESH LIME

The southern region of Spain is the birthplace of this refreshing summer favorite. The sweetness of plump ripened tomatoes mingles with the fresh flavors of garden vegetables, cilantro, and a splash of balsamic vinegar. Toss 4 ounces cooked shrimp in each serving, add a salad, and you have lunch.

Recipe by Cheryl Forberg, RD

1 large red bell pepper

2 large tomatoes or 6 plum tomatoes (about 1 pound)

1 large cucumber, peeled, halved lengthwise, and seeded

½ medium yellow onion

1 cup tomato juice

½ cup chopped fresh cilantro, without stems

¼ cup balsamic vinegar

2 tablespoons fresh lime juice

Salt and pepper to taste

Roast the whole red pepper under a broiler or over a gas flame, turning occasionally, until the skin blisters and chars all over. Place in a bowl, cover, and allow to steam to loosen the skin, or place in a paper bag until it is just cool enough to handle. Carefully peel away the skin and remove the seeds. Cut the pepper into medium dice and set aside.

Cut half of the tomatoes, half of the cucumber, and half of the onion into 1-inch pieces and transfer to the bowl of a food processor or a blender jar. Add the roasted bell pepper and process to a puree. Transfer to a medium mixing bowl. Add the tomato juice, cilantro, and vinegar. Seed the remaining tomato. Cut the tomato, cucumber, and onion into medium dice and add to the gazpacho.

Refrigerate until chilled. Just before serving, add the lime juice and season with salt and pepper. Serve well chilled. For a less chunky gazpacho, thin with additional tomato juice.

Makes 4 (1½-cup) servings

Per serving: 63 calories, 2 g protein, 14 g carbohydrates, less than 1 g fat (0 g saturated), 0 mg cholesterol, 3 g fiber, 15 mg sodium

Amy Hildreth's Diet Tip

Take your favorite recipes and modify them so they're healthy. That way you won't feel as if you're denying yourself.

SUZY PRESTON'S RANCH-STYLE "SPAGHETTI" MARINARA

Flavorful spaghetti squash can always be found in the kitchen at the ranch as a creative replacement for white pasta. Add turkey meatballs and a salad for a complete meal.

Olive oil spray

1 medium spaghetti squash (about 1½ pounds)

2 cups low-fat marinara sauce

2 tablespoons chopped fresh basil or parsley

2 tablespoons grated Romano or Parmesan cheese

Preheat the oven to 375°F. Lightly coat a baking sheet with olive oil spray. Wash the squash, cut in half lengthwise, and remove the seeds. Pierce the outside of each half a few times with a fork. Place the squash cut side down on the baking sheet. Bake until very tender when tested with a fork, about 45 minutes. Cool slightly.

Meanwhile, heat the marinara sauce in a medium saucepan over medium heat. Keep warm.

Using the tines of a fork, rake the spaghetti-like threads of squash into a mixing bowl. There should be about 3 cups of spaghetti squash. Discard the squash rind. Pour the hot marinara over the squash and toss gently. Divide the "spaghetti" among 4 serving plates and garnish with the basil or parsley and cheese.

Makes 4 servings

Per serving: 114 calories, 4 g protein, 18 g carbohydrates, 4 g fat (1 g saturated), 2 mg cholesterol, 4 g fiber, 574 mg sodium

Melinda Suttle's Diet Tip

Load up on veggies with every meal, including breakfast.

DANA DESILVIO'S YOGURT PARFAIT

*If you don't have fresh strawberries, other berries work
well in this refreshing treat. And if berries are out of season,
dried berries will also work, but use only 2 tablespoons.*

¼ cup diced fresh
  strawberries

2 tablespoons low-fat
  granola

1 cup (8 ounces) low-fat
  vanilla yogurt

1 fresh mint sprig

Combine the strawberries and granola in small mixing bowl and stir
to combine. Spoon half of the mixture into a serving bowl or parfait
glass and spoon the yogurt on top. Sprinkle the remaining granola-
strawberry mixture on top. Garnish with the fresh mint.

Makes 1 serving

Per serving: 253 calories, 13 g protein, 44 g carbohydrates, 4 g fat (2 g
saturated), 11 mg cholesterol, 2 g fiber, 172 mg sodium

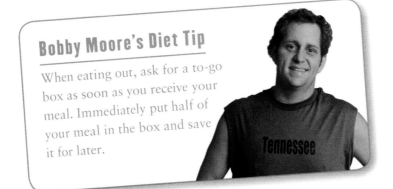

Bobby Moore's Diet Tip

When eating out, ask for a to-go
box as soon as you receive your
meal. Immediately put half of
your meal in the box and save
it for later.

Enjoy a "Cheat Meal"

A cheat meal once a week will help you stay on track in the long run. Why? It helps you keep from feeling deprived. It also gives you the opportunity to take a meal "off" and keeps you motivated to stay on the Biggest Loser program.

Keep in mind this is a cheat meal, not a cheat day. And there is one rule for the cheat meal. Be sure to eat your starch/breads with your protein entrée. So if you go out to a restaurant, don't just dive into the breadbasket. Wait until your entrée arrives. Then have that piece of bread.

Portion Power

As you begin the Biggest Loser diet, you'll want to weigh or measure your servings using a scale and measuring cups. If you're eating out and don't have

Bill Germanakos's Diet Tip

Don't skip any meal, especially breakfast; and figure out calories, burned and consumed.

access to a scale and measuring cup, you can take portion control into your own hands—literally. One cup of whole grains, vegetables, or fruit, for example, is about the size of your clenched fist; 1 protein serving is roughly the size of your hand. You won't have to weigh and measure forever. In a few short weeks, you'll be able to eyeball the correct portions. And once your portions slim down, so will your body.

Foods That Sabotage Your Diet

If you're determined to be your own "Biggest Loser," but find yourself caving in to cravings, it could be that your food choices are partially sabotaging your efforts. Eating certain foods will make you so hungry that you'll feel hollow inside. We call these *appetite-stimulating foods*. These include any food that has been stripped of its fiber such as white bread; foods that turn to sugar quickly in the body such as white potatoes; and foods loaded with sugar, starch, and fat. Some examples are:

- White bread
- White pasta
- White potatoes
- Pastries

(continued on page 166)

Dining Out Strategies from Bob Harper

Does your diet have to go into a tailspin at restaurants? Absolutely not, says Biggest Loser trainer Bob Harper. Here are his tips to prevent dining out disasters:

Fast food: It can be done. You can figure out a way to eat healthy at a fast food restaurant. These days every fast food place has salads, so here's what to do:

- Order one salad—or even two if you are hungry—and your favorite burger or sandwich "without the bun." Then make yourself a big salad with plenty of protein from your sandwich. It makes a difference. You will feel full and will have avoided the fries and the buns. As far as the salad dressing, you get 2 tablespoons of whatever it is you want and toss the rest.

- If salads aren't your thing, fine, go with your sandwich, without the bun and absolutely no mayo or special sauce of any kind. Hold off on the cheese and stay away from the fries and you could make it work. If it's fried, look away.

- Grilled chicken is always on menus now. Stay away from the fish, because it's probably fried. I know you like the fries—I do, too—but we are on a mission to lose weight and those fries are only going to get in the way of our progress.

Chinese: Chinese food is so good but so fattening. Here's the drill:

- Anything you want on the menu must be steamed! Whatever sauce comes with what you want, ask for it on the side and you get 2 tablespoons of it. You will get the taste you are looking for, but you have the control of how much sauce you have.

- After you have put the 2 tablespoons on your entrée, have the waiter take the sauce away to avoid any further "dipping." You won't feel deprived, because it will taste like you want it to, but your food won't be drowning in sauce.

- Stay away from the white rice and words like *stir-fried* or *egg roll* and by all means absolutely no fried rice.

Italian: This can be a little tricky because when you go to an Italian restaurant you are probably in the mood for pasta or pizza. Well, you can't—sorry!

- Go to the entrées and stick with all protein such as fish, chicken, or red meat. Request that the veggies be steamed and that the sauce for the veggies or protein be, you guessed it, "on the side."

- Get that breadbasket out of arm's reach. Try getting a small side of pasta sauce and put 2 tablespoons on your main meal. You will get that Italian taste that you want. It's a good little trick and it does work for fulfilling a craving.

Mexican: For starters, tell the waiter to not bring those chips to your table! I love them and could eat every basket they bring to me. Then:

- Instead, place an order for corn tortillas and dip them into your salsa. This is the same thing as the chips except that they're not fried, and they will satisfy your desire to dip.

- Instead of refried beans, ask for black beans—and no sour cream, no guacamole, no flour tortillas, no crispy taco shells. Okay, now that we have gone through all the "no's," let's turn to what you can order.

- Fajitas are a great choice since the meat is grilled and your veggies are included. It's also fine to order burritos and tacos, but ask for the filling only. What I do is order three or four tacos—beef or chicken—and combine the meat fillings with a big salad! There you go: a big taco salad without anything crunchy except the lettuce.

- No salad dressing required in a Mexican restaurant, because you have all that good salsa . . . Olé!

- Doughnuts
- Cookies
- Cakes, pies, and other sugary baked goods
- Candy and candy bars
- Potato chips and other packaged and fried snacks

Why do these foods give you that irresistible urge to raid the fridge or pantry? It has to do with their composition. The more fiber that is removed from a food, the harder and more rapidly the food hits your bloodstream. The sugar and refined starch it contains causes your blood sugar to soar sky high. In response to that sugar surge, your body churns out insulin—so much that it drives your blood sugar below where it was before you ate anything. When blood sugar is that low, you feel tired and hungry, and in need of another quick pickup—often in the form of something sweet. These ups and downs, coupled with the wrong food choices, can wreak havoc on your attempts to manage your weight. When a food contains both

Isabeau Miller's Diet Tip

Have healthy snacks nearby when you work out. That way you can take a break, and don't have to stop your momentum entirely.

fat and sugar, as many of the foods listed above do, it can be downright addictive, since many of us crave the taste of fat and sugar.

The key, of course, is to avoid appetite-stimulating foods—and make a habit of reaching for natural, wholesome, high-fiber foods and snacks instead. These whole foods are digested more slowly, causing fewer spikes in your blood sugar. What's more, they tame your hunger, rather than drive it wild with those crazy blood sugar ups and downs. Trust us, before long, you'll lose your sugar/fat/starch tooth and be in better control of your cravings.

There you have it—the Biggest Loser diet for big weight loss. Once you start following this diet—conscious of the food you put into your body—and gradually make the changes needed for healthier

Marty Wolff's Diet Tip

Reduced-fat peanut butter is my secret. It ain't too bad!

nutrition, you'll be amazed at how much better you look and feel. Just take it meal by meal, day by day. Every time you choose to eat healthy, you're a success, and success breeds success. Notice and celebrate every success, no matter how small. When you do that, you'll attract more of the same, and before you know it, you'll have what you desire: a trim, healthy body, the positive habits to maintain your weight loss for life, and a lot of self-respect in the process.

TRAINER TIP:
JILLIAN MICHAELS

Try to avoid "bad" carbs even if your body can tolerate a higher ratio of carbs. Bad carbs are processed grains and refined sugars. Complex or good carbs include whole grains, legumes, nuts, fruits, veggies, and so forth.

Avoid trans-fat (man-made fat). You can identify trans fats on a food label as "partially fractionated" or "hydrogenated oils."

With 13 grams of sugar per cup, milk is loaded with sugar. Try to get sugar-free milk at the market instead.

Appendix
Training Logs

Trainng Log: Beginner Routine #1

Photocopy or fill in the charts below to track your progress as you move through the program. Be sure to list the weights used and repetitions completed.

The Warmup

EXERCISE	TIME COMPLETED
Step Touches	
Arm Raises	
Simulated Jump Rope	
Shoulder Rolls	
Neck Rolls	
Marching in Place	

Upper-Body Exercises

EXERCISE	WEIGHT USED	REPS/TIME COMPLETED
Biceps Curls		
Triceps Dips		
Dead Lifts		
Chest Flies		
Shoulder Presses		
Overhead Pullovers		

Total Sets Completed: _____

Patty Gonzalez's Exercise Tip

Smile during the tough times or when you want to give up. Change up your routine often, to avoid boredom.

Core Exercises

EXERCISE	WEIGHT USED	REPS/TIME COMPLETED
Crunches		
Oblique Crunches		
Captain's Chair		
Plank		
Back Extensions		

Total Sets Completed: _____

Lower-Body Exercises

EXERCISE	WEIGHT USED	REPS/TIME COMPLETED
Lunges		
Thigh Adductions		
Step-Ups		
Reverse Lunges with Leg Lifts		
Calf Raises		

Total Sets Completed: _____

The Cooldown

EXERCISE	TIME COMPLETED
Calf Stretch	
Hamstring Stretch	
One-Arm Reach-Across	
Hip Flexor Stretch	
Triceps Stretch	
Quad Stretch	
Child's Pose	
Low Back and Glute Stretch	

Training Log: Beginner Routine #2

Photocopy or fill in the charts below to track your progress as you move through the program. Be sure to list the weights used and repetitions completed.

The Warmup

EXERCISE	TIME COMPLETED
Step Touches	
Arm Raises	
Simulated Jump Rope	
Shoulder Rolls	
Neck Rolls	
Marching in Place	

Upper-Body Exercises

EXERCISE	WEIGHT USED	REPS/TIME COMPLETED
Hammer Curls		
Triceps Kickbacks		
Dead Lifts		
Chest Presses		
T-Raises		
Bent-Over Row		

Total Sets Completed: _____

Core Exercises

EXERCISE	WEIGHT USED	REPS/TIME COMPLETED
Bicycle Maneuver		
Half Roll-Ups		
Vertical Leg Crunches		
Side Plank		
Hip Extensions		

Total Sets Completed: _____

Lower-Body Exercises

EXERCISE	WEIGHT USED	REPS/TIME COMPLETED
Squats		
Plie Squats		
Static Wall Squats		
Reverse Lunges with Leg Lifts		
Calf Raises		

Total Sets Completed: _____

The Cooldown

EXERCISE	TIME COMPLETED
Calf Stretch	
Hamstring Stretch	
One-Arm Reach-Across	
Hip Flexor Stretch	
Triceps Stretch	
Quad Stretch	
Child's Pose	
Low Back and Glute Stretch	

Training Log: Beginner Routine #3

Photocopy or fill in the charts below to track your progress as you move through the program. Be sure to list the weights used and repetitions completed.

The Warmup

EXERCISE	TIME COMPLETED
Step Touches	
Arm Raises	
Simulated Jump Rope	
Shoulder Rolls	
Neck Rolls	
Marching in Place	

Upper-Body Exercises

EXERCISE	WEIGHT USED	REPS/TIME COMPLETED
Biceps Curls		
Triceps Kickbacks		
Dead Lifts		
Push-Ups		
Shoulder Presses		
Overhead Pullovers		

Total Sets Completed: _____

Neil Tejwani's Exercise Tip

If your nipples start hurting from your shirt rubbing while working out, use body lube.

Core Exercises

EXERCISE	WEIGHT USED	REPS/TIME COMPLETED
Crunches		
Reverse Crunches		
Half Roll-Ups		
Wood Chops		
Back Extensions		

Total Sets Completed: _____

Lower-Body Exercises

EXERCISE	WEIGHT USED	REPS/TIME COMPLETED
Wall Squats with Stability Ball		
Side Lunges		
Bridge Pose with Stability Ball		
Side Steps		
Calf Raises		

Total Sets Completed: _____

The Cooldown

EXERCISE	TIME COMPLETED
Calf Stretch	
Hamstring Stretch	
One-Arm Reach-Across	
Hip Flexor Stretch	
Triceps Stretch	
Quad Stretch	
Child's Pose	
Low Back and Glute Stretch	

Training Log: Intermediate Routine #1

Photocopy or fill in the charts below to track your progress as you move through the program. Be sure to list the weights used and repetitions completed.

The Warmup

EXERCISE	TIME COMPLETED
Step Touches	
Arm Raises	
Simulated Jump Rope	
Shoulder Rolls	
Neck Rolls	
Marching in Place	

Upper-Body Exercises

EXERCISE	WEIGHT USED	REPS/TIME COMPLETED
Biceps Curls		
Triceps Dips		
Dead Lifts		
Chest Flies		
Shoulder Presses		
Overhead Pullovers		

Total Sets Completed: _____

Core Exercises

EXERCISE	WEIGHT USED	REPS/TIME COMPLETED
Crunches		
Oblique Crunches		
Captain's Chair		
Plank		
Back Extensions		

Total Sets Completed: _____

Lower-Body Exercises

EXERCISE	WEIGHT USED	REPS/TIME COMPLETED
Lunges		
Thigh Adductions		
Step-Ups		
Reverse Lunges with Leg Lifts		
Calf Raises		

Total Sets Completed: _____

The Cooldown

EXERCISE	TIME COMPLETED
Calf Stretch	
Hamstring Stretch	
One-Arm Reach-Across	
Hip Flexor Stretch	
Triceps Stretch	
Quad Stretch	
Child's Pose	
Low Back and Glute Stretch	

Training Log: Intermediate Routine #2

Photocopy or fill in the charts below to track your progress as you move through the program. Be sure to list the weights used and repetitions completed.

The Warmup

EXERCISE	TIME COMPLETED
Step Touches	
Arm Raises	
Simulated Jump Rope	
Shoulder Rolls	
Neck Rolls	
Marching in Place	

Upper-Body Exercises

EXERCISE	WEIGHT USED	REPS/TIME COMPLETED
Hammer Curls		
Triceps Kickbacks		
Dead Lifts		
Chest Presses		
T-Raises		
Bent-Over Row		

Total Sets Completed: _____

David Griffin's Exercise Tip

Never fall out of your routine, always keep it up! Constantly change your routine to keep things interesting. The Biggest Loser fitness plan gives you the options to do this.

Core Exercises

EXERCISE	WEIGHT USED	REPS/TIME COMPLETED
Bicycle Maneuver		
Half Roll-Ups		
Vertical Leg Crunches		
Side Plank		
Hip Extensions		

Total Sets Completed: _____

Lower-Body Exercises

EXERCISE	WEIGHT USED	REPS/TIME COMPLETED
Squats		
Plie Squats		
Static Wall Squats		
Reverse Lunges with Leg Lifts		
Calf Raises		

Total Sets Completed: _____

The Cooldown

EXERCISE	TIME COMPLETED
Calf Stretch	
Hamstring Stretch	
One-Arm Reach-Across	
Hip Flexor Stretch	
Triceps Stretch	
Quad Stretch	
Child's Pose	
Low Back and Glute Stretch	

Training Log: Intermediate Routine #3

Photocopy or fill in the charts below to track your progress as you move through the program. Be sure to list the weights used and repetitions completed.

The Warmup

EXERCISE	TIME COMPLETED
Step Touches	
Arm Raises	
Simulated Jump Rope	
Shoulder Rolls	
Neck Rolls	
Marching in Place	

Upper-Body Exercises

EXERCISE	WEIGHT USED	REPS/TIME COMPLETED
Biceps Curls		
Triceps Kickbacks		
Dead Lifts		
Push-Ups		
Shoulder Presses		
Overhead Pullovers		

Total Sets Completed: _____

Core Exercises

EXERCISE	WEIGHT USED	REPS/TIME COMPLETED
Crunches		
Reverse Crunches		
Half Roll-Ups		
Wood Chops		
Back Extensions		

Total Sets Completed: _____

Lower-Body Exercises

EXERCISE	WEIGHT USED	REPS/TIME COMPLETED
Wall Squats with Stability Ball		
Side Lunges		
Bridge Pose with Stability Ball		
Side Steps		
Calf Raises		

Total Sets Completed: _____

The Cooldown

EXERCISE	TIME COMPLETED
Calf Stretch	
Hamstring Stretch	
One-Arm Reach-Across	
Hip Flexor Stretch	
Triceps Stretch	
Quad Stretch	
Child's Pose	
Low Back and Glute Stretch	

Training Log: Advanced Routine #1

Photocopy or fill in the charts below to track your progress as you move through the program. Be sure to list the weights used and repetitions completed.

The Warmup

EXERCISE	TIME COMPLETED
Step Touches	
Arm Raises	
Simulated Jump Rope	
Shoulder Rolls	
Neck Rolls	
Marching in Place	

Upper-Body Exercises

EXERCISE	WEIGHT USED	REPS/TIME COMPLETED
Biceps Curls		
Triceps Dips		
Dead Lifts		
Chest Flies		
Shoulder Presses		
Overhead Pullovers		

Total Sets Completed: _____

Jez Luckett's Exercise Tip

Until you physically drop or are done with the workout, don't stop! You can do it even if you think you can't.

Core Exercises

EXERCISE	WEIGHT USED	REPS/TIME COMPLETED
Crunches		
Oblique Crunches		
Captain's Chair		
Plank		
Back Extensions		

Total Sets Completed: _____

Lower-Body Exercises

EXERCISE	WEIGHT USED	REPS/TIME COMPLETED
Lunges		
Thigh Adductions		
Step-Ups		
Reverse Lunges with Leg Lifts		
Calf Raises		

Total Sets Completed: _____

The Cooldown

EXERCISE	TIME COMPLETED
Calf Stretch	
Hamstring Stretch	
One-Arm Reach-Across	
Hip Flexor Stretch	
Triceps Stretch	
Quad Stretch	
Child's Pose	
Low Back and Glute Stretch	

Training Log: Advanced Routine #2

Photocopy or fill in the charts below to track your progress as you move through the program. Be sure to list the weights used and repetitions completed.

The Warmup

EXERCISE	TIME COMPLETED
Step Touches	
Arm Raises	
Simulated Jump Rope	
Shoulder Rolls	
Neck Rolls	
Marching in Place	

Upper-Body Exercises

EXERCISE	WEIGHT USED	REPS/TIME COMPLETED
Hammer Curls		
Triceps Kickbacks		
Dead Lifts		
Chest Presses		
T-Raises		
Bent-Over Row		

Total Sets Completed: _____

Core Exercises

EXERCISE	WEIGHT USED	REPS/TIME COMPLETED
Bicycle Maneuver		
Half Roll-Ups		
Vertical Leg Crunches		
Side Plank		
Hip Extensions		

Total Sets Completed: _____

Lower-Body Exercises

EXERCISE	WEIGHT USED	REPS/TIME COMPLETED
Squats		
Plie Squats		
Static Wall Squats		
Reverse Lunges with Leg Lifts		
Calf Raises		

Total Sets Completed: _____

The Cooldown

EXERCISE	TIME COMPLETED
Calf Stretch	
Hamstring Stretch	
One-Arm Reach-Across	
Hip Flexor Stretch	
Triceps Stretch	
Quad Stretch	
Child's Pose	
Low Back and Glute Stretch	

Training Log: Advanced Routine #3

Photocopy or fill in the charts below to track your progress as you move through the program. Be sure to list the weights used and repetitions completed.

The Warmup

EXERCISE	TIME COMPLETED
Step Touches	
Arm Raises	
Simulated Jump Rope	
Shoulder Rolls	
Neck Rolls	
Marching in Place	

Upper-Body Exercises

EXERCISE	WEIGHT USED	REPS/TIME COMPLETED
Biceps Curls		
Triceps Kickbacks		
Dead Lifts		
Push-Ups		
Shoulder Presses		
Overhead Pullovers		

Total Sets Completed: _____

Jim Germanakos's Exercise Tip

When you think you've done all the reps you can, do three more!

Core Exercises

EXERCISE	WEIGHT USED	REPS/TIME COMPLETED
Crunches		
Reverse Crunches		
Half Roll-Ups		
Wood Chops		
Back Extensions		

Total Sets Completed: _____

Lower-Body Exercises

EXERCISE	WEIGHT USED	REPS/TIME COMPLETED
Wall Squats with Stability Ball		
Side Lunges		
Bridge Pose with Stability Ball		
Side Steps		
Calf Raises		

Total Sets Completed: _____

The Cooldown

EXERCISE	TIME COMPLETED
Calf Stretch	
Hamstring Stretch	
One-Arm Reach-Across	
Hip Flexor Stretch	
Triceps Stretch	
Quad Stretch	
Child's Pose	
Low Back and Glute Stretch	

Bibliography

American College of Sports Medicine. "Selecting and using home weights." www.acsm.org.

American Council on Exercise (ACE). "ACE-sponsored study reveals best and worst abdominal exercises." May 14, 2001. www.acefitness.org

Borsheim, E., and R. Bahr. "Effect of exercise intensity, duration and mode on post-exercise oxygen consumption." *Sports Medicine* 33, no. 14 (2003): 1037–60.

Braun, W. A., et al. "Acute EPOC response in women to circuit training and treadmill exercise of matched oxygen consumption." *European Journal of Applied Psychology* 94, no. 5–6 (August 2005): 500–504.

Burke, L. M. "Nutrition for post-exercise recovery." *Australian Journal of Science and Medicine in Sport* 21, no. 1 (1997): 3–10.

Carlson, C. R., et al. "Muscle stretching as an alternative relaxation training procedure." *Journal of Behavioral Therapy and Experimental Psychiatry* 21, no. 1 (March 1990): 29–38.

Ivy, J. L. "Glycogen resynthesis after exercise: Effect of carbohydrate intake." *International Journal of Sports Medicine* 19, Suppl. 2 (June 1998): S142–S145.

Koh-Banerjee, P., et al. "Prospective study of the association of changes in dietary intake, physical activity, alcohol consumption, and smoking with 9-y gain in waist circumference among 16,587 US men." *American Journal of Clinical Nutrition* 78, vol. 4 (October 2003): 719–27.

Mairorana, A., et al. "Combined aerobic and resistance exercise improves glycemic control and fitness in type 2 diabetes." *Diabetes Research and Clinical Practice* 56, vol. 2 (May 2002): 115–23.

Margareta Eriksson, K., et al. "A randomized trial of lifestyle intervention in primary healthcare for the modification of cardiovascular risk factors." *Scandinavian Journal of Public Health* 34, vol. 5 (2006): 453–61.

Norvell, N., and D. Belles. "Psychological and physical benefits of circuit weight training in law enforcement personnel." *Journal of Consulting and Clinical Psychology* 61, vol. 3 (June 1993): 520–27.

Romine, I. J., et al. "Lavendar aromatherapy in recovery from exercise." *Perceptual and Motor Skills* 88. (1999): 756–58.

Schuenke, M. D., et al. "Effect of an acute period of resistance exercise on excess post-exercise oxygen consumption: implications for body mass management." *European Journal of Applied Psychology* 86, vol. 5 (March 2002): 411–17.

Sites, C. K., et al. "Effect of a daily supplement of soy protein on body composition and insulin secretion in postmenopausal women." *Fertility and Sterility* (April 3, 2007). Epub ahead of print.

Watts, K., et al. "Exercise training normalizes vascular dysfunction and improves central adiposity in obese adolescents." *Journal of the American College of Cardiology* 43, vol. 10 (May 19, 2004): 1823–27.

Whitehurst, M. A. "The benefits of a functional exercise circuit for older adults." *Journal of Strength and Conditioning Research* 19, vol. 3 (August 2005): 647–51.

Acknowledgments

When I was asked to work on another Biggest Loser book, I was honored but also very excited to be reunited with many of the same wonderful people I had worked with on *The Biggest Loser—The Weight-Loss Program to Transform Your Body, Health, and Life*. Thanks go to Amy Super, our editorial director, for her outstanding editing and creative ideas in organizing the content; Chad Bennett at Reveille, who once again was so efficient in coordinating the project and pulling together all the information we needed; Mark Koops, managing director, Creative Affairs of Reveille, for being so committed to another Biggest Loser book; and Cindy Chang at NBC Universal for all her far-ranging, behind-the-scenes work on the book's behalf.

Also, I would like to express my appreciation to our other editors, Nancy N. Bailey, our project editor, and Deri Reed, our freelance copy editor, for their support, talent, and hard work. Thank you to Chris Gaugler, the interior designer, and Chris Rhoads, the cover designer, for designing a beautiful book; and to Liz Perl, publisher, Rodale Books, and Nancy Hancock, executive editor, Rodale Books, for their dedication to bringing this book together.

A special thank you to the cast members and trainers from every season of *The Biggest Loser*. It is through your example that so many millions of Americans have found the inspiration to master their bodies, attain self-confidence, and transform their lives.

Maggie Greenwood-Robinson, PhD
Dallas, Texas

Biggest Loser Experts

Michael Dansinger, MD, is an internal medicine physician who completed a nutrition research fellowship at Tufts University. He serves as the director of clinical studies and obesity research for the Atherosclerosis Research Laboratory within the Division of Endocrinology, Diabetes, and Metabolism at Tufts-New England Medical Center. Dr. Dansinger is the principal investigator of the widely publicized Tufts Popular Diet. He has been interviewed by numerous news organizations, and he lectures widely about popular diets and weight loss to medical and nonmedical audiences across the country.

Cheryl Forberg, RD, is a professional chef and the nutritionist for NBC's *The Biggest Loser.* A member of the opening team of the restaurant Postrio, Wolfgang Puck's first venture in northern California, Cheryl earned a degree in nutrition and clinical dietetics and an RD (registered dietitian) credential from the University of California at Berkeley. In 2005, she won the prestigious James Beard award for healthy recipe development. Cheryl is also a food and nutrition journalist, and her writing and recipes have appeared in many publications. Cheryl has authored or contributed to nine books.

Maggie Greenwood-Robinson, PhD, is a leading health and medical writer in the United States. She has authored or coauthored more than 40 books on nutrition, exercise, weight loss, brain fitness, and health issues such as cancer and diabetes. Among her most recent books are *Good Food versus Bad Food* and *The Bikini Diet.* She has a doctorate in nutritional counseling.

Bob Harper, trainer on *The Biggest Loser,* has traveled the world, empowering millions and sharing his successful holistic approach to fitness and weight loss. He is working on a program entitled *Diabetes & You: Step It Up to Get It Down—6.5 Steps toward Better Blood Sugar Control* to help people with type 2 diabetes control their blood sugar levels. His favorite activities include yoga, running, photography, and reading. According to Bob, the key to life is to realize that today is the first day of the rest of your life—and that you have the power to change anything you put your mind to. He lives in Los Angeles.

Robert Huizenga, MD, is considered one of the leading weight loss experts in the country today. As an associate professor of clinical medicine at UCLA, Dr. Huizenga has a busy medical practice that studies obesity-related issues. Formerly, Dr. Huizenga was the doctor for the Los Angeles Raiders and preisdent of the NFL Physician Society. Dr. Huizenga has repeatedly been interviewed as a health expert on many news programs. He has also been called as a medical expert in multiple high profile legal cases, including the O. J. Simpson, anabolic steroid, and Botox trials. He has had recurrent roles as a writer, correspondent, and advisor on numerous TV shows.

Kim Lyons, trainer on *The Biggest Loser,* is a graduate of Colorado State University and the National Academy of Sports Medicine. She is an International Federation of Bodybuilders (IFBB) pro competitor and the recipient of multiple national and international awards, including the Miss Galaxy title. Kim has graced the cover and pages of numerous magazines including *Oxygen, Muscle and Fitness,* and *Self.* Kim enjoys traveling, cooking, and extreme sports, and she is the author of *Your Body, Your Life.* She lives in Hermosa Beach, California, with her husband, Gunter Schlierkamp.

Jillian Michaels, trainer on *The Biggest Loser,* holds personal training certificates from the National Endurance and Strength Training Association (NESTA) and the American Fitness Association of America (AFAA). She is a contributor to *Redbook* and *Cosmo Girl,* and she is an ambassador for the American Cancer Society and an AOL Fitness Coach. Jillian has a passion for motorcycle racing, and her favorite pastime is racing the track at Willow Springs on her Ducati 1098s.

Index

Underscored page references indicate boxed text and tables. **Boldface** references indicate photographs.

Diabetes
exercise and, 4–5, 102
risk factors for, 3, 51
stretching and, 89
Diet. *See also* Biggest Loser Diet
exercise and, 14–15
Dining out. *See* Eating out
Dinner, suggestions for, 156, <u>157</u>
Doctor approval, for exercise program, <u>22</u>
Donahue, Lezlye, **10**, **10**
Dumbbells, 5–6, 11, 105

Eating out, <u>162</u>, 163, <u>164–65</u>
Eisenbarth, Jennifer, <u>7</u>, 7, <u>159</u>, **159**
Emotional changes, from circuit
training, 2
Emotional eating, 88
EPOC (excess post-exercise oxygen
consumption), 3, 106
Equipment, exercise, 5–7, 105
Erector spinae muscles, 50
Exercise mat, 6
Exercise(s). *See also* Circuit training;
Strength training; Workouts
assessing fitness for, <u>22</u>
avoiding boredom with, <u>170</u>, <u>176</u>
consistency with, <u>29</u>, 145
diet and, 14–15
difficulty of, x
doctor approval of, <u>22</u>
effectiveness of, ix–x
equipment for, 5–7, 105
health benefits from, xix, 102–3
hydration for, 12–14
increasing, for weight loss, <u>9</u>
partner for, <u>3</u>, <u>103</u>
proper form for, 9, 10–11, <u>104</u>, 106
safety with, 8–10
warmup improving, 18–19
Exercise tubing, 6, 105

Failure mentality, xxiii
Fast-food choices, <u>164</u>
Fat, body, xix, 14
Fat burning, 1, 2, 3, 18, 144
Fats, dietary, in Biggest Loser Diet,
148–49, 154
Fiber-rich foods, <u>51</u>, 166
Fiber-stripped foods, 163, 166
Fioravanti, Dave, xxii
Fish and shellfish, in Biggest Loser Diet,
151

Fitness level, finding, for workouts,
103–5
Flexibility, 86, <u>87</u>
Food preparation methods, 158
4-3-2-1 Biggest Loser Pyramid, 149–55,
149
Fruit juices, 14, 151
Fruits, in Biggest Loser Diet, 149, 150,
151
Fudgsicle, <u>150</u>
Full roll-up, 59
Fun activities, <u>21</u>, <u>91</u>, 103
Functional fitness or strength, xviii, 1,
4, 34, 49, 68, 102

Gazpacho
Icy Gazpacho with Fresh Lime, 160
Germanakos, Bill, <u>163</u>, **163**
Germanakos, Jim, **54**, <u>54</u>, **186**, <u>186</u>
Gluconeogenesis, 148
Gluteal muscles, 68
Glycosylation end products, with
diabetes, 89
Goal outfit, <u>33</u>
Gonzalez, Patty, <u>11</u>, **11**, <u>91</u>, **91**, <u>170</u>, **170**
Grains, whole, in Biggest Loser Diet,
153–54
Griffin, David, <u>98</u>, **98**, <u>178</u>
Growth hormone, fat burning and, <u>99</u>
Gym, joining, <u>5</u>
Gym buddy, <u>3</u>, <u>103</u>

Hadden, Julie, <u>40</u>, **40**, <u>77</u>, 77, <u>155</u>, **155**
Half roll-ups, 59, **59**
Hammer curls, 36, **36**
Hamstrings, 68
Hamstring stretch, 92, **92**
Hansen, Heather, xx, xxi, 19, <u>97</u>, **97**
Harper, Bob, <u>19</u>, **19**, <u>47</u>, <u>65</u>, 67–68, 88,
<u>103</u>, 144, 145, <u>164–65</u>, **164**
Hawk, Phil, <u>57</u>, 57, <u>71</u>, 71
Headaches, exercise-induced, 20
Healthy fats, 148–49
Healthy life, rewards from, xiii
Heart disease, 3, 5, 51, 102, 103
Heart rate monitor, 7, 105
Heart rhythms, warmups and, 19
Hibbard, Kai, xvi, <u>xvi</u>, **xvi**, xxii, <u>81</u>, **81**
High blood pressure, exercise
preventing, 102
Hiking, <u>19</u>
Hildreth, Amy, xx, <u>160</u>, **160**

Hip extensions, 63, **63**
Hip flexor stretch, 94, **94**
Hoover, Matt, <u>xxii</u>, **xxii**, <u>2</u>, **2**, <u>18</u>, **18**
Huizenga, Robert, xix, xvii
Hunger, 13, 163, 166
Hydration, 12–14, <u>155</u>

Immune system, 19–20, 107
Injuries, 10, <u>18</u>, 89
preventing, 9–10, 19, 34, 68, <u>92</u>
Insulin, 51, <u>99</u>, 166
Insulin resistance, xvi, 51
Intermediate circuit routines, 105, **112–
15**, **124–27**, **136–39**
training logs for, <u>176–81</u>
Italian food choices, <u>165</u>

Joint health, 10, 86
Juices, fruit, 14, 151

Kelly, Ryan, <u>4</u>, **4**
Knees, protecting, 68
Kortesmaki, Adrian, xx, xxi, <u>21</u>, **21**, <u>65</u>,
<u>102</u>, **102**
Kramer, Poppi, <u>xx</u>, **xx**, xxi–xxii

Latissimus dorsi, 33
Lean mass, loss of, xix
Legs
exercises for (*see* Lower-body
exercises)
warmup for, 21
Life span, exercise increasing, 102
Lime
Icy Gazpacho with Fresh Lime, 160
Lisenby, Jerry, <u>104</u>
Low back and glute stretch, 98, **98**
Lower-body exercises
in advanced circuit routines, **118**,
130, **142**
in beginner circuit routines, **110**, **122**,
134
benefits of, 67–68
bridge pose with stability ball, 82, **82**
calf raises, 79, **79**
in intermediate circuit routines, **114**,
126, **138**
lunges, 71, **71**
muscles targeted by, 68
plié squats, 74, **74**

SHED THE POUNDS WITH
THE BIGGEST LOSER ON DVD!

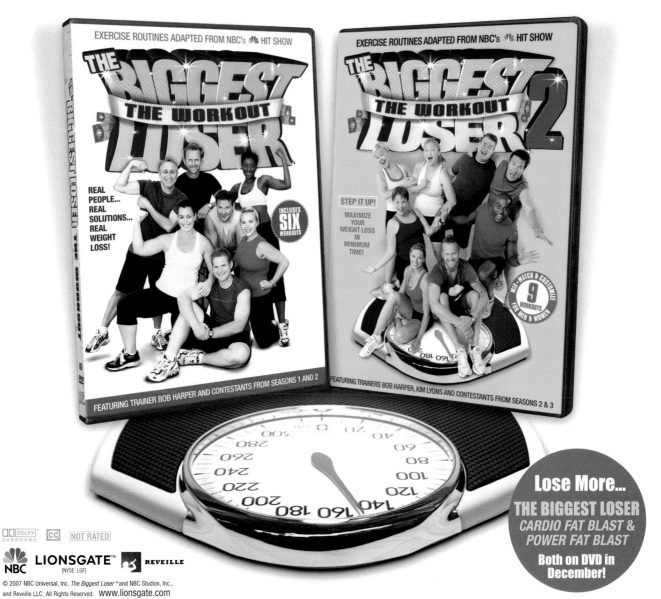

EXERCISE ROUTINES ADAPTED FROM NBC's HIT SHOW

THE BIGGEST LOSER
THE WORKOUT

REAL PEOPLE... REAL SOLUTIONS... REAL WEIGHT LOSS!

INCLUDES SIX WORKOUTS

FEATURING TRAINER BOB HARPER AND CONTESTANTS FROM SEASONS 1 AND 2

EXERCISE ROUTINES ADAPTED FROM NBC's HIT SHOW

THE BIGGEST LOSER 2
THE WORKOUT

STEP IT UP!
MAXIMIZE YOUR WEIGHT LOSS IN MINIMUM TIME!

MIX, MATCH & CUSTOMIZE 9 WORKOUTS FOR MEN & WOMEN

FEATURING TRAINERS BOB HARPER, KIM LYONS AND CONTESTANTS FROM SEASONS 2 & 3

Lose More...
THE BIGGEST LOSER
CARDIO FAT BLAST &
POWER FAT BLAST
Both on DVD in December!

DOLBY SURROUND   CC   NOT RATED

NBC   LIONSGATE™ [NYSE: LGF]   REVEILLE

© 2007 NBC Universal, Inc. The Biggest Loser™ and NBC Studios, Inc., and Reveille LLC. All Rights Reserved.   www.lionsgate.com

MADE TO FIT

Stay on track with the online program, diet and exercise logs and get fit with the trainers you love from the show - Bob Harper and Kim Lyons.

WWW.BIGGESTLOSERCLUB.COM/FIT

the experts, the teams, the challenges – it's all online

Don't Miss The Biggest Loser

 NBC